MANAGEMENT OF ENTERPRISE CRISES IN JAPAN

Japanese Management and International Studies
(ISSN: 2010-4448)

Editor-in-Chief: Yasuhiro Monden *(Tsukuba University, Japan)*

Published

Vol. 1   Value-Based Management of the Rising Sun
edited by Yasuhiro Monden, Kanji Miyamoto, Kazuki Hamada,
Gunyung Lee & Takayuki Asada

Vol. 2   Japanese Management Accounting Today
edited by Yasuhiro Monden, Masanobu Kosuga,
Yoshiyuki Nagasaka, Shufuku Hiraoka & Noriko Hoshi

Vol. 3   Japanese Project Management:
KPM — Innovation, Development and Improvement
edited by Shigenobu Ohara & Takayuki Asada

Vol. 4   International Management Accounting in Japan:
Current Status of Electronics Companies
edited by Kanji Miyamoto

Vol. 5   Business Process Management of Japanese and Korean Companies
edited by Gunyung Lee, Masanobu Kosuga, Yoshiyuki Nagasaka &
Byungkyu Sohn

Vol. 6   M&A for Value Creation in Japan
edited by Yasuyoshi Kurokawa

Vol. 7   Business Group Management in Japan
edited by Kazuki Hamada

Vol. 8   Management of an Inter-Firm Network
edited by Yasuhiro Monden

Vol. 9   Management of Service Businesses in Japan
edited by Yasuhiro Monden, Noriyuki Imai, Takami Matsuo &
Naoya Yamaguchi

Vol. 10 Management of Enterprise Crises in Japan
edited by Yasuhiro Monden

Japanese Management and International Studies – Vol. 10

MANAGEMENT OF ENTERPRISE CRISES IN JAPAN

editor

Yasuhiro Monden

Tsukuba University, Japan

World Scientific

NEW JERSEY · LONDON · SINGAPORE · BEIJING · SHANGHAI · HONG KONG · TAIPEI · CHENNAI

Published by

World Scientific Publishing Co. Pte. Ltd.

5 Toh Tuck Link, Singapore 596224

USA office: 27 Warren Street, Suite 401-402, Hackensack, NJ 07601

UK office: 57 Shelton Street, Covent Garden, London WC2H 9HE

Library of Congress Cataloging-in-Publication Data
Monden, Yasuhiro, 1940–
   Management of enterprise crises in Japan / by Yasuhiro Monden.
    pages cm. -- (Japanese management and international studies, ISSN 2010-4448 ; vol. 10)
   Includes bibliographical references and index.
   ISBN 978-9814508506
   1. Management--Japan. 2. Crisis management--Japan. 3. Natural disasters--Economic
aspects--Japan. 4. Business failures--Japan. I. Title.
   HD70.J3M5957 2014
   658.4'770952--dc23

                        2013027368

British Library Cataloguing-in-Publication Data
A catalogue record for this book is available from the British Library.

In-house Editors: Sandhya Venkatesh/Chitralekha Elumalai

Typeset by Stallion Press
Email: enquiries@stallionpress.com

Printed in Singapore

Japan Society of Organization and Accounting (JSOA)

President
Gunyung Lee, Niigata University, Japan

Vice Presidents
Kazuki Hamada, Kwansei Gakuin University, Japan
Yoshiyuki Nagasaka, Konan University, Japan

Directors
Henry Aigbedo, Oakland University, USA
Shufuku Hiraoka, Soka University, Japan
Mahfuzul Hoque, University of Dhaka, Bangladesh
Noriko Hoshi, Hakuoh University, Japan
Tomonori Inooka, Kokushikan University, Japan
Chao Hsiung Lee, National Chung Hsing University, Taiwan
Yoshiteru Minagawa, Nagoya Gakuin University, Japan
Kozo Suzuki, Tokyo Metropolitan Government, Japan

Founder & Editor-in-Chief
Japanese Management and International Studies
Yasuhiro Monden, Tsukuba University, Japan

Auditor
Kanji Miyamoto, Osaka Gakuin University, Japan

Assistant Managers
Naoya Yamaguchi, Niigata University, Japan
Hiromasa Hirai, Takasaki City University of Economics

Mission of JSOA and Editorial Information
For the purpose of making a contribution to the business and academic communities, the Japan Society of Organization and Accounting (JSOA) is committed to publishing the book series, entitled *Japanese Management and International Studies*, with a refereed system.

Focusing on Japan and Japan-related issues, the series is designed to inform the world about research outcomes of the new "Japanese-style management system" developed in Japan. However, as the series title suggests, it also promotes "*International Studies*" on the interface of managerial competencies between Japan and other countries that include Asian countries as well as Western countries under the globalized business activities of Japanese companies.

Research topics included in this series are management of organizations in a broad sense (including the business group or networks) and the accounting that supports the organization. More specifically, topics include business strategy, business models, organizational restoration, corporate finance, M&A, environmental management, operations management, managerial & financial accounting, manager performance evaluation, reward systems. The research approach is interdisciplinary, which includes case studies, theoretical studies, normative studies and empirical studies, but emphasizes real world business.

Each volume contains the series title and a book title which reflects the volume's special theme.

Our JSOA's board of directors has established an editorial board of international standing. In each volume, guest editors who are experts on the volume's special theme serve as the volume editors.

The details of JSOA are shown in its by-laws contained in the homepage: http://jsoa.sakura.ne.jp/english/index.html

Contents

Preface   xi

About the Editor   xv

List of Contributors   xvii

PART 1: Business Turnaround under Public Financial Support   1

1. How Can All Stakeholders "Share the Burden" of Solving Damage Liability and Turnaround of Nuclear Power Electric Company?   3
   Yasuhiro Monden and Masaaki Imabayashi

2. The Turnaround of Japan Airlines   31
   Naoyuki Kaneda

PART 2: Private Turnaround to Cope with the Business Crisis   47

3. The Choice that Samsung Electronics Made in the Monetary Crisis of 1997   49
   Hyeun Kyoung Song and Gunyung Lee

4. Activities of Cross-Functional Teams (CFTs) in Nissan: Considering from Revitalization Activities and their Results   65
   Kazuki Hamada

5. Overcoming the Business Crisis by Applying Capital Cost Management: Case Study of the Panasonic Group   83
   Shufuku Hiraoka

PART 3: Coping with Business Crisis Applying the New Managerial Accounting　　95

6. Basic Theory of Management for the Business Crisis　　97

   Akira Miyama

7. Profit Management Model to Overcome the Enterprise Crisis　　109

   Noriyuki Imai

PART 4: Supply-Chain Management after the Disasters and TPS after Business Crisis　　123

8. Robust Supply-Chain Management for the Disasters: Based on the Product Design Architectures　　125

   Yasuhiro Monden and Rolf G Larsson

9. Management of Humanitarian Supply Chains in Times of Disaster　　149

   Yoshiteru Minagawa

10. Creation and Continuous Development of the Toyota Production System for Solving Current and Potential Business Crises　　165

    Shino Hiiragi

Index　　183

Preface

As Japan has suffered huge calamities caused by both the earthquakes and tsunami, including damages to the nuclear power plants of Tokyo Electricity Company on March 11, 2011 which in turn has led to tremendous crises to Japanese enterprises, I decided to share my thoughts on how to solve the encountering crisis in Japan. Actually, this disaster happened successively after the Leman brother's economic shock and the 20-year long depression since 1991 bubble burst in Japan. These two preceding economic problems are also part of enterprise crises. Because the great disasters and the preceding economic problems have been affecting countries in recent times the knowledge of Japanese experiences in coping with these crises will be useful to the readers throughout the world.

Thus, this volume has the theme of the *Management of Enterprise Crises in Japan.* Let us clarify the meaning of the theme briefly. It is managing the rebirth or revival of enterprises that are on the edge of bankruptcy or business failure. (Thus, our research target is the business "crisis," rather than a business "risk.")

This is also rephrased as the "turnaround" management of an ailing firm. It may be categorized as the following two schemes:

(1) Route to reform of the financial structure.
(2) Route to reform the revenue creating structure.

When we see these two schemes from the view point of accounting, the first topic is to reform the balance sheet by decreasing the debt and increasing the shareholders' equity. The second topic is to create business activities that yield profits in the bottom line.

Recent examples include the rebirth problem faced by Japan Air Lines. Hottest topics include (a) management of Tokyo Electric Power Company and (b) managing how to indemnify (or compensate) for the damages caused by the nuclear power plants of Tokyo Electric Power Company.

Also, the great earthquakes and tsunami which hit eastern Japan on March 11, 2011 have caused tremendous crises in the local agricultural and fishery industries. The supply chain of the automobile industry has also much suffered by these big disasters. Thus, this volume also discusses measures to strengthen the supply chain under disasters. We should build robust supply chains by enhancing the commonization or standardization (i.e., modularity) of parts of each product.

This volume covers broad case studies and explores their generalization to derive some theories. In summary, it consists of the following five PARTS:

- **PART 1: Business Turnaround under Public Financial Support:**
  - How Can All Stakeholders "Share the Burden" of Solving Damage Liability and Turnaround of Nuclear Power Electric Company?
  - The Turnaround of Japan Airlines

- **PART 2: Private Turnaround to Cope with the Business Crisis:**
  - The Choice that Samsung Electronics Made in the Monetary Crisis of 1997
  - Activities of Cross-Functional Teams (CFTs) in Nissan: Considering from Revitalization Activities and their Results
  - Overcoming the Business Crisis by Applying Capital Cost Management: Case Study of the Panasonic Group

- **PART 3: Coping with Business Crisis Applying the New Managerial Accounting:**
  - Basic Theory of Management for the Business Crisis
  - Profit Management Model to Overcome the Enterprise Crisis

- **PART 4: Supply-Chain Management after the Disasters and TPS Innovation after Business Crisis:**
  - Robust Supply-Chain Management for the Disasters: Based on the Product Design Architectures
  - Management of Humanitarian Supply Chains in Times of Disaster
  - Creation and Continuous Development of the Toyota Production System for Solving Current and Potential Business Crises.

Acknowledgments

I am very grateful to Ms. Juliet Lee Ley Chin, senior consulting editor of the Social Sciences in the World Scientific Publishing Company for her invaluable advice to make this volume a reality. Further, Ms. Divya Srikanth and Ms. E. Chitralekha, the desk editors, are acknowledged for their handling the manuscripts. The contributing authors of this volume will be amply rewarded when their new ideas or knowledge contribute to the business management and managerial accounting, thereby being of relevant use to people, governments, and policy makers around the world.

Yasuhiro Monden
Volume editor
July 16, 2013

About the Editor

Yasuhiro Monden is Professor Emeritus at the University of Tsukuba and currently serving as Visiting Professor at the Global MBA Program of the Nagoya University of Commerce and Business, both in Japan. He has majored in production management and managerial accounting. He received his PhD from the University of Tsukuba, where he also served as Chairperson of the Institute and Dean of the Graduate Program of Management Sciences and Public Policy Studies.

Monden has gained valuable practical knowledge and experience from his research and related activities in the Japanese automobile industry. He was instrumental in introducing the Just-In-Time (JIT) production system to the United States. His book, *Toyota Production System* (Engineering and Management Press: IIE, 1983, 1993, 1998, and 2011) published in English, is recognized as a JIT classic; it was awarded the 1984 Nikkei Prize by the *Nikkei Economic Journal.*

Monden was a Visiting Professor at the State University of New York at Buffalo in 1980–1981, at California State University, Los Angeles in 1991–1992 and at Stockholm School of Economics, Sweden in 1996. He is also a board member and advisor for the Production and Operations Management Society (POMS) and an international director of the Management Accounting Section of the American Accounting Association.

Other English-language books written by Monden include: *Cost Reduction System: Target Costing and Kaizen Costing* (Productivity Press, 1995); *Japanese Management Accounting* (Productivity Press, 1989); *Value-Based Management of the Rising Sun* (World Scientific Publishing Company, 2006); *Management of an Inter-Firm Network* (World Scientific Publishing Company, 2012).

Monden's professional activities in the business world include practical guidance on JIT system and strategic cost management in Singapore and Thailand as an expert of JICA (Japan International Cooperation Agency), an agency of the Japanese Ministry of Foreign Affairs, and his service as a committee member of the second examination of Certified Public Accountant in Japan.

List of Contributors

Kazuki Hamada
Professor, Kwansei Gakuin University
School of Business Administration, Japan
1-1 Uegahara, Nishinomiya, Hyogo 662-8501, Japan
Ph.D. in Management Science and Engineering from Tsukuba University
bft88135@kwansei.ac.jp

Shino Hiiragi
Associate Professor
Department of System Innovation, Faculty of Engineering
Management of Technology, Graduate School of Science and Engineering
Yamagata University, Japan
4-3-16 Jonan, Yonezawa City, Yamagata 992-8510, Japan
Doctor of Business Administration and Computer Science from
Aich Institute of Technology
s_hiiragi@nifty.com

Shufuku Hiraoka
Professor, Faculty of Business Administration, Soka University, Japan
1-236 Tangi-cho, Hachioji-city, Tokyo 192-0087, Japan
Ph.D. in Business Administration from Meiji University
shiraoka@soka.ac.jp

Masaaki Imabayashi
Professor, Faculty of Business Administration, Mejiro University, Japan
4-31-1 Nakaochiai, Shinjuku, Tokyo 161-8539, Japan
Master of Engineering from Tokyo University of Science
m-imbys@dream.ocn.ne.jp

Noriyuki Imai
Vice President, Toyota Financial Services Corporation
6-1 Ushijima-cho, Nishi-ku, Nagoya 451-6015, Japan
Visiting Professor, Meijo University, Japan
1-501 Shiogamaguchi, Tenpaku-ku, Nagoya 468-8502, Japan

Ph.D. in Business from Meijo University
silverstone@mta.biglobe.ne.jp

Naoyuki Kaneda
Professor, Faculty of Economics, Gakushuin University, Japan
1-5-1 Mejiro, Toshima-ku, Tokyo 171-8588, Japan
Ph.D. in Industrial Administration (Accounting) from
Carnegie Melon University, USA
naoyuki.kaneda@gakushuin.ac.jp

Rolf G Larsson
Associate Professor, School of Economics and Management,
Lund University, Sweden
John Ericssons väg 3, 223 63 Lund, Sweden
Doctor of Business Administration, Växjo University, Sweden
Rolf.Larsson@fek.lu.se

Gunyung Lee
Professor, Faculty of Economics, Niigata University, Japan
8050 Ikarashi 2-no-cho, Niigata City 950-2181, Japan
Ph.D. in Management Science and Engineering from Tsukuba University
lee@econ.niigata-u.ac.jp

Yoshiteru Minagawa
Professor, Faculty of Commerce, Nagoya Gakuin University
1350 Kamishinano-cho, Seto, Aichi 480-1298, Japan
Ph.D. in Economics from Nagoya University
minagawa@ngu.ac.jp

Akira Miyama
Professor, School of Business Administration,
Kwansei Gakuin University, Japan
1-1 Uegahara, Nishinomiya, Hyogo 662-8501, Japan
Ph.D. in Business Administration from Kwansei Gakuin University
amiyamakira@kcc.zaq.ne.jp

Yasuhiro Monden
Professor Emeritus of Tsukuba University, Japan
2-28-11 Umezono, Tsukuba-shi, Ibaraki, 305-0045, Japan
Ph.D. in Management Science and Engineering from Tsukuba University
yasuhirom@mail2.accsnet.ne.jp

Hyeun Kyoung Song
Assistant Professor, School of Management,
Dongyang Mirae University, Korea
303 ho, Hyosungkwan, 445, Gyeongin-ro, Guro-gu, Seoul, Korea (152-714)
Ph.D. in Business Administration from Sogang University, Korea
hksongde@gmail.com

PART 1

Business Turnaround under Public Financial Support

1

How Can All Stakeholders "Share the Burden" of Solving Damage Liability and Turnaround of Nuclear Power Electric Company?

Yasuhiro Monden
University of Tsukuba

Masaaki Imabayashi
Mejiro University

1　Research Theme

The March 11, 2011, accident at the Tokyo Electric Power Company's (TEPCO) Fukushima Daiichi Nuclear Power Station created two crises for the entire Kanto region — damage from radioactive contamination and power supply shortages. Solving these two crises is an urgent task that all of Japan, not just TEPCO, must take seriously. The nation confronts two key issues: (1) assisting accident victims; and (2) ensuring a stable electricity supply (i.e., by rebuilding the company). This chapter sheds light on how all interested parties (i.e., stakeholders) can "share the burden" of solving these two issues.

We first explore how all parties — not only TEPCO but also the Japanese government, other power companies, and TEPCO's investors (including shareholders and financial institutions) — can share the burden of compensating private and corporate victims for damages caused by the nuclear accident. The task is to construct a formal scheme for sharing the compensation burden among all interested parties. This chapter begins by investigating this damage compensation issue (see Sec. 2).

A post-accident turnaround strategy is needed to prevent the risk of TEPCO's failure. On April 27, 2012, a little over a year after the Great East

Japan Earthquake caused the accident, the Nuclear Damage Liability Facilitation Fund (the "Fund") and TEPCO jointly announced a Comprehensive Special Business Plan (the "Business Plan"), which was subsequently approved on May 9, 2012, by Yukio Edano, Japan's Minister of Economy, Trade, and Industry. This plan appears to leave unanswered the question of what strategy should be adopted to "share the burden" of TEPCO's restructuring among its interested parties (stakeholders). Thus, the second issue this chapter deals here is TEPCO's restructuring (see Sec. 3).

Common to both issues is the need for stakeholders to share the "pain" of the Japanese government and TEPCO in procuring funds for compensation and turnaround while reducing costs and increasing revenue (by raising electricity prices) in order to cover the costs. Therefore, in its conclusion (Sec. 4), this chapter discusses a theory for the ways of "sharing the burden" that apply to both damage compensation and business turnaround.

2   Sharing the Burden of TEPCO's Damages Liability

We will first investigate how the many interested parties concerned can best share the burden of the compensation costs for damages caused by the nuclear accident.

2.1   *Overview of the Nuclear Damage Liability Act*

Here, we review the key sections of Japan's 1961 Nuclear Damage Liability Act (i.e., Act on Compensation for Nuclear Damage) in order to describe the systems by which individuals and companies who suffer damages through accidents at nuclear power stations in Japan are compensated.

Section 1 of the law states the law's purpose as being (1) to pay compensation to victims quickly in order to protect them and (2) to secure a stable supply of electricity.

Section 3 defines the strict liability of nuclear power plant operators, stating that electric power companies bear "unlimited liability." Here, "strict liability" means that the business operator is assigned liability without fault and is subject to unlimited compensation. Thus, the business operator bears unlimited liability.

However, a proviso states that a nuclear operator shall be liable for damages "except in the case where the damage is caused by a grave natural disaster of an exceptional character or by an insurrection." In such cases, then, the nuclear power plant operators are exempt from liability for damages. Nevertheless, the Japanese government has interpreted this proviso as envisaging a meteor strike or war (according to senior officials of the Ministry of Culture, Sports, Science, Education, and Technology). Also this Tohoku region has repeatedly experienced the similar scale earthquakes and Tsunami in the past. Thus does not believe it applies to the Fukushima Daiichi Nuclear Power Plant accident.

Section 6 stipulates two measures for damage compensation: (1) compensation can be made through "nuclear damage insurance," but this is not available for the Fukushima accident because the insurance has an earthquake exclusion; (2) under the Contract for Indemnification of Nuclear Damage Compensation, the state provides monetary compensation in case of an earthquake, volcanic eruption, or tsunami, where a nuclear power plant has been operating normally. The sum to be paid is only ¥120 billion. Since this is not nearly enough to cover the liability, Section 16 (described below) has been applied.

Section 16 provides that the government shall provide the required assistance to a nuclear power station operator when nuclear damage has occurred and the amount of the liability for damage compensation to be borne by the nuclear power station operator under Section 3 exceeds the "compensation measure amount" of ¥120 billion (per site) set out in Section 6.

2.2 "State assistance" for Nuclear Damage Liability and the Role of the Nuclear Damage Liability Facilitation Fund

To implement the provisions of Section 16, the government newly enacted the Nuclear Damage Liability Facilitation Fund Act on August 10, 2011, in light of the nuclear accident (refer to The Facilitation Fund Act, Act No. 94, August 10, 2011; Yamauchi, May 25, 2011; Morita, July 13, 2011; *The Nikkei*, July 29, 2011; August 3, 2011). This Act stipulated measures ensuring aid to all victims by requiring the government provide the necessary assistance to nuclear power station operators whenever nuclear damage in excess of the ¥120 billion compensation measure amount per nuclear accident site is incurred and when the operators are unable to pay the entire compensation amount using their own financial resources.

This new Act became the basis of the state's provision of compensation. The purpose, though, is to assist victims, not to provide power station operators some sort of exemption from unlimited liability. However, the measure does go beyond mere victim protection by preventing TEPCO from bankruptcy owing to insolvency.

Meanwhile, TEPCO's balance of corporate bonds has risen to ¥5 trillion, and its financing balance (bank loan balance) has risen to ¥4 trillion. Without state assistance, TEPCO bonds were expected to crash; this would have hurt banks, as the balance of TEPCO's loans would have had to be written off as non-performing, making it difficult for the company to procure new financing.

To resolve this problem, the support scheme described below was devised.

The damages liability borne by TEPCO and its shareholders are to be shouldered by the public in the form of a cash injection from the government funded by tax revenues. To enable this, the government established the Nuclear Damage Liability Facilitation Fund (hereafter abbreviated as the Facilitation Fund) by issuing government bonds. The Fund is an approved corporation founded in accordance with the Nuclear Damage Liability Facilitation Fund Act enacted in August 10, 2011. It is capitalized at only ¥14 billion, with ¥7 billion from the government and ¥7 billion from nuclear power station operators (e.g., electric power companies), and is a corporation jointly established by the private sector and the state. However, the framework allows the government to issue up to ¥5 trillion

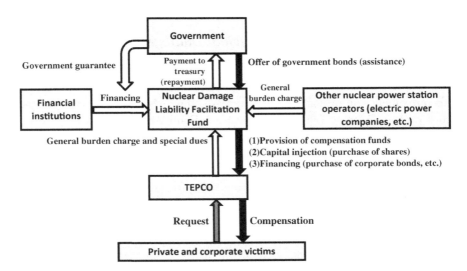

Fig. 1.   TEPCO public assistance scheme.
(Adapted and revised from *The Nikkei*, July 29, 2011.)

in government bonds to the Facilitation Fund. The Facilitation Fund can then monetize these bonds in the market and issue compensation funds to TEPCO. Moreover, when the Facilitation Fund receives financing from banks as needed, the government will guarantee the debts (see Fig. 1)

Furthermore, under the current Nuclear Damage Liability Act (revised in 2009), if the compensation required exceeds the ¥120 billion provided as a "damage compensation measure" for each nuclear power station site (this time case has No. 1 and No. 2 stations of nuclear accidents), the Nuclear Damage Liability Facilitation Fund will provide "funding assistance" to the electric power company that caused the accident in the following ways:

(1) Provision of compensation funds,
(2) Capital injection (receiving shares), and
(3) Financing (e.g., purchasing corporate bonds).

Of these, (1) refers specifically to funding for TEPCO's damage liability, while (2) and (3) are meant to achieve TEPCO's turnaround.

All electric power companies have provided to the Fund a "general burden charge," a preliminary source of funds. However, since this contribution is insufficient, the Fund will also monetize national bonds issued by the government (public funds) and use them to supply compensation funds to TEPCO as "special funding assistance" (see Fig. 1).

2.3 Burden charges for TEPCO and other electric power companies and repayment of public funds

Under the Nuclear Damage Liability Act, hurriedly enacted on August 10, 2011 to cope with TEPCO's nuclear accident, nuclear power plant operators are required to jointly provide a "general burden charge" to the Facilitation Fund. The charge is shared among 11 companies: 9 electric power companies, The Japan Atomic Power Company, and Japan Nuclear Fuel Limited. The burden charges are determined according to the output size of the companies' nuclear reactors and thus depend on each company's capacity to bear them. Under the system, if another electric power company were to cause a man-made nuclear accident, the same assistance scheme would be applied, with the burden charge acting as a sort of insurance premium and the Facilitation Fund as a sort of insurance company assisting electric power companies in paying compensation (*The Nikkei*, March 2, 2012). The general burden charge can be counted as part of the "cost" of the electricity price of each electric power company (the so-called "full cost").

To receive special funding assistance, TEPCO must submit to the government a Special Business Plan detailing its management rationalization measures after the Fund is launched. If TEPCO receives assistance, it must pay not only the "general burden charge" paid by other electric power companies but also "special dues." Unlike the general burden charge, the funds for the special dues may not be included in electricity fees but must be derived through restructuring or other means. Accordingly, TEPCO will begin paying these special dues after the fiscal year ending in March 2015.

The Fund will use these general burden charges and special dues as financial resources to repay public funds to the state over the long term. Although the public funds issued by the government to the Facilitation Fund are not formally the debt to TEPCO, they might be interpreted as being repaid to the government through the Facilitation Fund via the general burden charge and special dues paid by TEPCO over many years (see Fig. 1).

2.4   *Compensation scheme based on market principles and "state responsibility"*

Because the "measure prevents TEPCO from bankruptcy due to becoming insolvent," as mentioned in Sec. 2.2, the scheme is not considered a so-called "compensation scheme based on market principles." Were TEPCO to face insolvency, market principles would require that the Corporate Reorganization Act be applied, and without aids from the government all stakeholders of the market must autonomously compensate victims for damage liability and restruct TEPCO. In other words, shareholders made to take responsibility, creditors (financial institutions) forced to write off their loans, and plants makers of nuclear power reactors and general constructors forced to take product liability. Afterward, TEPCO would need to restructure itself, and the government would provide assistance only to meet shortfalls in the funds needed to compensate victims (see Saito, 2011; Nomura, 2011; Fukui, 2011, Oshima, 2011). However, these market principles have not been adopted.

In many countries outside of Japan such as America, England, and France, the liability of nuclear power station operators is limited to the amount provided by damage compensation measures (i.e., liability insurance and government guarantee); the means of preventing operator collapse is thus incorporated into the legal system. Japan's Nuclear Damage Liability Act (as like as Germany and Switzerland) assigns no-fault, unlimited liability to operators. Overseas scholars from the U.S. have argued that the state's responsibility should be clarified: as the nuclear power business is a product of the state's own policy, the state should bear primary responsibility for assisting victims and should establish a fund for this purpose using tax revenue.

To materialize the framework for state assistance accordingly, the August 2011 enactment of the Nuclear Damage Liability Facility Fund Act includes a "supplementary provision" in which the government states that it would work to fundamentally revise the 1961 Nuclear Damage Liability Act stipulating TEPCO's unlimited liability. This effort has not yet borne fruit. Moreover, the Facilitation Fund Act added a clause stating that "shareholder cooperation will be sought," leaving the question of what burden should be borne by "interested parties," including shareholders, to future revisions.

Japan's nuclear power plants were introduced in line with state energy policy, and their operation was entrusted to regionally monopolistic electric power companies provided with funds by financial institutions through loans and acquisitions of shares and corporate bonds. After the most recent accident, the state's responsibility as a commissioner, the electric power companies' responsibility as undertakers, and shareholders' and investors' responsibilities have been left vaguely defined. The immediate focus has been on resolving the two priority issues — assisting victims and ensuring a stable electricity supply (through business reform). To achieve this, a scheme has been created for providing practical state assistance via the Facilitation Fund. In commenting on its own responsibility, the government has stated only that "the state is bearing the social responsibility that follows from its having promoted a nuclear power policy up until now (clause 2 of the Facilitation Fund Act)."

2.5   *TEPCO'S accounting treatment of compensation funds issued from the Facilitation Fund*

The Facilitation Fund has already decided to provide TEPCO with ¥1.58 trillion in assistance for compensation funds. In TEPCO's accounting treatment of these funds, money received from the Facilitation Fund is recorded on TEPCO's income statement as "special profit" (clause 69 of Facilitation Fund Act). This is to offset on the income statements against "expenses for nuclear damage compensation" under "special loss." Thus, the compensation funds provided from the Facilitation Fund are not treated as liabilities, but as assistance just like a donation. On the surface, then, TEPCO is not accumulating debt; in reality, though, the general burden charge and special dues that TEPCO will pay to the Facilitation Fund will be used by the Fund as a financial resource to repay the state (*The Nikkei*, August 11, 2011).

For example, in its quarterly financial report for April 1 to June 30, 2011, TEPCO recorded a special loss for refugees' psychological suffering, and thus a consolidated net loss of ¥571.7 billion resulted. The "offered funds" can continue to be treated as special profit described above, allowing TEPCO to cover the losses accruing from paid compensation.

2.6 *Summary: Sharing the burden of nuclear damage compensation*

This section has identified five stakeholders (interested parties) who provide many of the funds TEPCO uses to pay compensation for nuclear damages, as shown in Fig. 1:

- The Japanese government (or nation): issues government bonds to the Facilitation Fund as the ultimate sponsor.
- Nuclear Damage Liability Facilitation Fund: issues compensation funds to TEPCO. (The Facilitation Fund is merely an agent of the government.)
- Financial institutions (shareholders and creditors): finance the Facilitation Fund.
- Other electric power companies: pay the general burden charge.
- TEPCO: manages the offered compensation funds and pays the burden charges to the Facilitation Fund to repay the compensation funds.

This chapter has shed light on the structure used to share the burden among these five stakeholders.

3 Sharing the Burden of TEPCO's Restructuring among Stakeholders

3.1 *Relationship between company restructuring and stakeholders*

Following the accident at its Fukushima Daiichi Nuclear Power Station, TEPCO required a turnaround strategy to avoid failing. On April 27, 2012, a little over a year after the Great East Japan Earthquake caused the accident, the Facilitation Fund and TEPCO jointly announced a Comprehensive Special Business Plan. (*The Nikkei*, April 28, 2012) (hereafter abbreviated as the "Business Plan"), which was subsequently approved on May 9, 2012, by Yukio Edano, Japan's Minister of Economy, Trade, and Industry.

This section investigates how the burden of TEPCO's restructuring is to be shared among stakeholders under the Business Plan.

Business restructuring usually requires the following:

(1) A financial structure strategy (or a financial structure reform strategy), and
(2) A business structure strategy (or a profit structure reform strategy).

The financial structure reform mentioned in (1) refers to a structural reform of the capital composition of a company's balance sheet. This generally requires a contraction of liabilities and an expansion of net assets or shareholder equity:

(A) The former often requires creditor financial institutions to bear the burden of writing off debts.
(B) The latter often requires shareholders to purchase newly issued shares collectively to bolster shareholder equity. For TEPCO, however, the government (the taxpayer) is to purchase the new shares as a means of injecting owner's capital.

The profit structure reform of (2) is meant to bring the net income on the company's income statement back into the black. This usually entails strategies for cost reduction and sales revenue expansion. The "cost reduction" requires that the following functional cost reduction strategies be implemented for each of the company's stakeholders:

(a) Reduce the cost of procuring raw materials, materials, and components from *suppliers*.
(b) Reduce the labor costs incurred by *plant employees* (e.g., through layoffs or wage reductions) to reduce plant processing costs.
(c) Reduce labor costs incurred by *administrative employees* (as above) to reduce general management costs.
(d) Request that *creditors* (financial institutions) and *shareholders* bear some of the burden to reduce capital costs (i.e., interest payments and dividends).

(e) Reduce payments of incentives to *sales dealers* to reduce sales and advertising costs.

(f) A public utility company such as electric power company cannot help "increasing the sales revenues" by asking *consumers* (*customers*) to bear part of the burden by accepting an increase in sales prices. A private-sector for-profit enterprise must expand sales by taking on new businesses or developing new products or markets to cultivate new customers.

The reforms in (a) through (f) above are intended to make up the loss on a non-profitable company's income statement and return it to profitability. As the equation below shows, it is clearly necessary to approach this effort from both the cost-cutting and sales expansion perspectives:

$$Amount\ of\ loss = total\ required\ cost\ reduction\ amount$$
$$+ sales\ revenue\ increase\ amount.$$

The top management decides the ratio at which these two aspects are balanced. If a loss is anticipated, the "total required cost reduction amount," which increases the burden on suppliers and employees, etc. will naturally be given greater weight than the amount of a price hike, because the total expenses are bigger than the total revenues in such a company. Once this "total required cost reduction amount" has been decided, it can be allocated among functional departments (i.e., company stakeholders) in accordance with the cost composition ratio of each functional cost item and the cost of each functional department making up the current total cost (the reforms carried out under President Carlos Ghosn at Nissan Motor Company, for example, were based on a similar approach).

In formulating the Business Plan, the Facilitation Fund (government) and TEPCO have settled on a primary policy of employing a so-called "turnaround procedure before bankruptcy" for TEPCO, which risks failure due to the formidable accident at the nuclear power station caused by the Great East Japan Earthquake. This procedure will introduce turnaround measures before TEPCO fails.

3.2 *Scheme for restructuring TEPCO*

As noted above, the general framework for restructuring a business comprises both balance sheet and income statement reforms. The scheme for restructuring TEPCO's business is shown in Fig. 2.

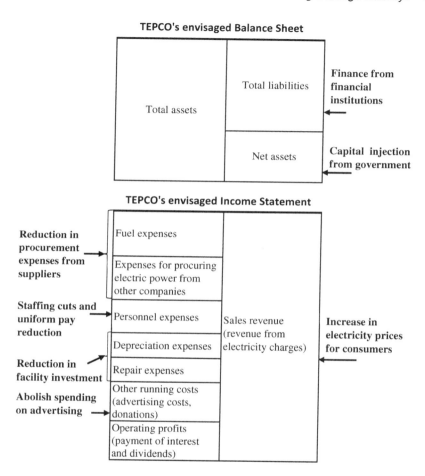

Fig. 2. Sharing the burden of TEPCO's restructuring among stakeholders.

Since TEPCO's turnaround is premised on the treatment before bankruptcy (as noted above), it raises the issue of what form TEPCO's state assistance would take. As explained in Sec. 1, the Facilitation Fund is an approved corporation based on the Nuclear Damage Liability Facilitation Fund Act created for the purpose of "ensuring swift and appropriate payment of compensation for nuclear damage and securing stable supplies of electricity by performing services such as issuing funds required for damage liability of a nuclear power station operator in the case where large-scale nuclear damage has occurred."

Under the scheme shown in Fig. 2, the Facilitation Fund will purchase most of TEPCO's shares, so that the government (the Facilitation Fund) will effectively control TEPCO as the parent company.

3.3 *Government involvement in TEPCO's restructuring*

Here, we examine the reasons behind the adoption of the "turnaround procedure before bankruptcy" in the Business Plan.

The government involves itself in business restructuring in one of two ways: "turnaround procedure after bankruptcy" or "turnaround procedure before bankruptcy."

An example of the former can be seen in the application of the "special public management" provision of the Financial Reconstruction Act (i.e., Act on Emergency Measures for the Revitalization of the Financial Functions enacted on October 16, 2010) for the former Long-term Credit Bank of Japan, Ltd., and Nippon Credit Bank, Ltd., both of which have swollen bad debts. In both cases, the government purchased all of the banks' shares for ¥0, rendering the shares held by existing shareholders valueless. In addition, ¥6.0 trillion in public funds was injected to cover the two banks' enormous losses. An example involving a business company is that of Japan Airlines Co., Ltd., which applied for the Corporate Reorganization Act in 2010. The state's Enterprise Turnaround Initiative Corporation of Japan injected ¥350 billion into Japan Airlines to purchase their newly issued stocks following a 100% capital reduction, thus temporarily nationalizing it (*The Nikkei*, April 28, 2012).

A prime example of effectively nationalizing a company through a "turnaround before bankruptcy" is that of Resona Holdings, Inc., in 2003. The government received Resona's preferred shares with voting rights for a stake of over 50%. *The Nikkei* (April 28, 2012) noted that this had a disadvantage: "over ¥800.0 billion of the total ¥3.0 trillion injected to Resona still remains uncollected, and since the turnaround procedure before bankruptcy does not allow the subject company to free itself of debts, it tends to take a long time to repay public funds." By comparison, in the case of Japan Airlines, to which the government's Enterprise Turnaround Initiative Corporation of Japan applied the turnaround procedure after bankruptcy, the company was able to achieve relisting relatively quickly, on September 19, 2012, in the second year after bankruptcy (*The Nikkei*, September 20, 2012).

The major difference between these two methods is, then: that in the turnaround procedure after bankruptcy, the existing shares become valueless and are delisted; whereas, in the turnaround procedure before bankruptcy, the shares' value declines through dilution (as the number of shares increases) but does not become zero, and nor are the shares delisted.

According to Nakayama (2012), the turnaround procedure before bankruptcy was selected for TEPCO because the company's liability for damage compensation was anticipated to run into several trillions of yen, and the company was believed destined for insolvency without government assistance. This would have posed a risk to the victims, who deserve top priority, because bankruptcy could have cut their damage compensation.

The government therefore established the Facilitation Fund and issued it with government bonds that can be monetized to assist TEPCO in paying compensation. Moreover, in accordance with the Business Plan, the Facilitation Fund received shares issued by TEPCO on July 31, 2012 (of approximately ¥1.0 trillion). As a result, the Facilitation Fund acquired more than half of TEPCO's total issued shares with voting rights; with the further receipt of shares allowing acquisition of voting rights, the Fund has the potential to control more than two-thirds of the voting rights (*The Nikkei*, July 31, 2012, and August 1, 2012).

3.4 *Schematic diagram of burden-sharing*

Here, we examine the allocation of TEPCO's post-accident burden and clarify the roles of the shareholders, the Facilitation Fund, the consumers who will bear price increases, and the financial institutions, etc.

3.4.1 *"Burden" of shareholders (existing shareholders and government [taxpayers])*

The effect of the Facilitation Fund's purchase of TEPCO shares is described below (*The Nikkei*, May 22, 2012).

To receive capital injections totaling ¥1.0 trillion, TEPCO issues a type of class share called "preferred shares." They issue two classes of preferred shares, differentiated based on whether or not they include voting rights, and the Facilitation Fund receives all of them. At the time of issuance, the Facilitation Fund controlled 50.11% of voting rights, substantially nationalizing TEPCO. Under the scheme for the preferred shares, TEPCO issues

1.6 billion shares of class A preferred stock with voting rights at ¥200 per share (totaling ¥320 billion) and 340 million shares of class B preferred stock without voting rights at ¥2000 per share (¥680 billion), with the Facilitation Fund receiving both issues. However, if TEPCO's Business Plan does not proceed as envisaged, the Facilitation Fund may convert the class B shares into class A shares to increase its voting rights share to 75.84%, thus increasing its involvement in the process. Conversely, if the turnaround proceeds as planned, the Facilitation Fund may lessen its involvement by converting the class A shares into class B shares.

The impact of this scheme on shareholders will be twofold. The benefit is that the company's financial status will be restored, allowing it to avoid insolvency. The drawback, however, is that the Facilitation Fund will control the majority of the voting rights, reducing those of the existing shareholders. Moreover, converting the preferred stock to common stock will lower the share price substantially. The price range for conversion to common stock is between ¥30 and ¥300, which changes in tandem with TEPCO's share price at the time of conversion. If, in the worst case, all ¥1.0 trillion of the preferred stock were converted to common stock at ¥30, the lowest end of this range, the number of issued common stock shares would rise by around 33.3 billion, diluting the value of the shares held by previous shareholders to around 1/20th of their former value.

3.4.2 *"Burden" of creditors (financial institutions)*

On April 28, 2012, when the Business Plan was announced by the Facilitation Fund and TEPCO, several financial institutions expressed their willingness to provide additional financing to TEPCO totaling ¥1.7 trillion (*The Nikkei*, April 28, 2012). In the Business Plan section entitled "(5) Strengthening Our Financial Standing 1) Requests to Financial Institutions," the following request to financial institutions appears: "Per discussions with the Facilitation Fund and TEPCO, all the Lenders will maintain TEPCO's credit line via refinancing efforts, etc., until we reach the stage where we will be able to procure financing independently through the corporate bond market, etc." The scheme comprises three pillars: new financing of ¥500.0 billion, an additional credit line of ¥400.0 billion if needed, and a roll-over of ¥170.0 billion to maintain the balance of loans extended to TEPCO. This shows that the scheme, which centers on the Facilitation Fund, is predicated on not allowing TEPCO to fail.

The plan also includes a request that lenders "promptly provide additional credit up to approx. ¥1 trillion...via provision of new loans and short term commitment lines." The abovementioned newspaper report notes that the Development Bank of Japan, Inc., and Sumitomo Mitsui Banking Corporation have both complied with these requests as TEPCO's transacting financial institutions.

According to the Business Plan, TEPCO's cash flow has seen cash and cash equivalents for the fiscal year ending March 31, 2012, decline by ¥1,077.7 billion year on year. This is almost the same as the abovementioned financing amount of three pillars. Therefore, the burden of the financial institutions appears to be providing financing to cover the net decrease in TEPCO's cash flow, with the government's scheme of "not allowing TEPCO to fail" serving as a kind of security.

3.4.3 *Burden of consumers: Electricity price increase*

While the injection of public funds is broadly borne by the nation's taxpayers, a more direct burden is the electricity price increases borne by the consumers of the Kanto region (i.e., Eastern Japan surrounding Tokyo). Electricity prices are calculated according to the following formula (Federation of Electric Power Companies of Japan, 2012):

$$
\begin{aligned}
\textit{Electricity price} = {} & \textit{Basic charge} \\
& + \textit{electric power unit charge} \times \textit{wage amount} \\
& \pm \textit{fuel cost adjustment unit charge} \times \textit{usage amount} \\
& + \textit{additional fee for promoting solar power generation.}
\end{aligned}
$$

Moreover, the basic and electric power unit charges are determined through the so-called "full cost method," which is based on the three principles of the Electricity Business Act: "cost basis," "fair compensation," and "fairness to electricity users."

Of these principles, cost basis is relevant to this chapter. This principle requires that the "rates are determined based on the *fair costs* incurred as a result of efficient management, added by the *fair profits*." A simplified version of the full cost method can be expressed by the following formula:

$$
\textit{Revenue from electricity charges} = \textit{full cost} + \textit{planned profit.}
$$

Here, "full cost" comprises such expenses as those for fuel, repairs, electric power procurement, depreciation, and personnel. The "planned profit," referred to as "business remuneration" (i.e., business return) in the Electricity Business Act, consists chiefly of the payment of interest and dividends that the electricity companies are required to procure funds from the creditors and shareholders for the construction and maintenance of electricity generation and transmission infrastructure. This dividend is an amount corresponding to the dividend payment as a disposal of the net income after tax. This planned profit is calculated by applying a certain rate (rate of the business return) to the amount of assets such as power stations and distribution networks. The rate has gradually declined and is currently set at 3%.

According to the Business Plan, the average full cost per year for fiscal 2012 through to fiscal 2014 is projected to be ¥5,723.1 billion, against projected total revenue from electricity charges of only ¥5,046.8 billion, leaving a shortfall of ¥676.3 billion. The plan proposes that this shortfall be covered by increases in electricity prices. However, this calculation factors in a contribution from a reduction in fuel expenses following the restart of the Kashiwazaki Kariwa Nuclear Power Station of TEPCO in April 2013. A delayed restart could cause TEPCO's balance of payments to further deteriorate.

The wording of the Business Plan makes clear that the rise in costs attributable to the sharp increase in fuel expenses following the stoppage of nuclear power stations is to be borne by users via electricity price increases.

Moreover, the Business Plan had aimed to increase prices for residential users by 10.28% after July 1, 2012. In the event, however, the government approved an increase of only 8.46% on July 25, 2012, to take effect on September 1, 2012 (*The Nikkei*, August 1, 2012).

This decision on the electricity price increase means that electricity bills for average households paying ¥7,000 per month will increase by ¥360 (*The Nikkei*, July 25, 2012). Reducing the price increase has made it even more difficult to put TEPCO on the road to a turnaround. The Business Plan had targeted an ordinary income of ¥91.6 billion for the fiscal year ending March 2014, but reducing the price increase has cut the target revenue by ¥81.3 billion down, a level that barely allows the company to remain profitable. If the company cannot become profitable in the fiscal year ending March 2014, it will have recorded three consecutive years of losses, and the financing extended to TEPCO by financial institutions will be deemed "non-performing debt," raising the danger of TEPCO's financing being terminated (*The Nikkei*, July 19, 2012).

3.4.4 *Burden of employees*

Labor expenses will be reduced by ¥1,275.8 billion over 10 years, while taking into consideration TEPCO's personnel system. This entails a personnel reduction that will see the number of employees as of April 1, 2011, reduced on a consolidated basis by approximately 7,400 employees by the end of March 2014. This includes a reduction of approximately 3,600 employees at the parent company. All employee salaries and bonuses have been reduced and will remain so until the end of fiscal 2012.

3.4.5 *Burden of suppliers*

The Business Plan aims to cut procurement expenses for materials and services by ¥664.1 billion over 10 years through a sweeping revision of the transaction structure (in a switch to open tenders). Power purchase and fuel procurement expenses will also be reduced by ¥198.6 billion over 10 years, while repair expenses and outsourcing expenses are to be reduced by slashing transactions of single tender contracts with subsidiaries and affiliates by 30%.

3.4.6 *Burden of local governments*

Because of their proximity to TEPCO's Fukushima Daiichi Nuclear Power Station, local governments, particularly the Fukushima prefecture and its municipalities, still face difficulty in ascertaining the extent of the damage, even in the second half of 2012, over 18 months after the accident. This, along with various issues concerning the future which have yet to be decided, have made it difficult even to calculate the damage costs accurately.

The damage costs comprise many categories, including emergency shelter for residents, decontamination, and the radioactive contamination of agricultural produce. Expenditures on these have likely been provisionally made by local governments. The Act on Emergency Measures Concerning Damage from the March 2011 Nuclear Accident (enacted on August 5, 2011) sets out a scheme for damage compensation, but the risk of new problems, such as health damage to residents that may continue over several decades, remains. In addition, local governments have borne non-financial burdens after the accident that cannot be quantified.

3.4.7 Burden of TEPCO and its management

The burden that TEPCO must bear comes in the form of the cost-cutting measures for its income statement items, as has been described above.

The responsibility of TEPCO's management, as a stakeholder, is described below.

The chairman and president of TEPCO resigned when the Business Plan was formulated to take responsibility as the manager of the company. The company has changed from having a traditional Japanese governance structure (thus being a "company with auditor") to being American-type structure of a "company with committees," with a general meeting of shareholders held in June of 2012. As a result, the board of directors was separated from executive functions for the board to be able to control the executives, and the majority of the directors are now outside directors. This has strengthened shareholders' governance on top management and has given greater control to the government, the majority shareholder.

Concerning TEPCO's organizational reforms, the July 30, 2012, *The Nikkei* reported seven key projects following the effective nationalization of the company. The first one of particular interest is "reforming the awareness of employees," while a noteworthy organizational reform is the introduction of an in-house company or divisional profit center system with three intra-companies to handle "retail," "transmission & distribution" of electric power, and "fuel & thermal generation." This will "allow for greater transparency in in-house transactions and thus enhance management discipline."

The plan for a "transmission & distribution" company is notable as a declaration of TEPCO's intention to implement a "generation-transmission split," whereby an electric power company separates its generation business from its transmission & distribution business. The generation-transmission split was one of the basic reform policies proposed by the Electricity System Reform Specialists Committee of the Japanese Ministry of Economy, Trade, and Industry on July 13, 2012 (*The Nikkei*, July 19, 2012). This kind of split increases the independence of the transmission and distribution division and separates its management from that of the generation division, which should encourage new operators to enter the industry, increasing competition and helping to control increase of electricity prices (Kikkawa, 2012).

3.5 *Summary: Sharing the burden of TEPCO's restructuring*

In conclusion, in a scheme centered on the Facilitation Fund, TEPCO appears unlikely to fail as long as the government can continue to pour compensation assistance and capital injection funds into the Facilitation Fund without limit. However, issuing government bonds in ¥1 trillion lots is effectively passing the bill to Japanese citizens despite the fact that government bonds were already ballooning before the earthquake. If Japanese citizens are unable to pay for the bill, it follows the nation's bankruptcy.

Moreover, additional fuel costs due to the suspension of other nuclear power stations are also being shouldered directly by consumers in the form of electricity price increases. The general charges on the electricity companies other than TEPCO will also be added on their "full costs" as a basis of electricity price determination. While there will be no burden on financial institutions if TEPCO repays its debts faithfully, future events may oblige them to bear the significant burden of writing the debts off. It would be difficult to apply the turnaround procedure after bankruptcy due to the need to pay compensation for the nuclear power station accident; the company will thus be required to accept cost-cutting measures, including painful internal restructuring that will affect employees.

The burden must thus be shared among the state (taxpayers), financial institutions, users (consumers), and TEPCO employees, who must accept tough restructuring measures. If any one of these fails to carry their "share of the burden," TEPCO's turnaround will be impossible, and the company will not survive.

4 Conclusion: A Theory on the Fair Allocation of the Burden of Compensation Funds and Turnaround Funds

For the survival of the organization (TEPCO) as a coalition of members of various stakeholders, each of them must contribute to sharing the burden. In this section, we conclude by considering what kind of burden allocation would be fair and secure the assent of the stakeholders who will share it.

4.1 *Barnard's organizational equilibrium theory*

Barnard's organizational equilibrium theory defines an organization as a coalition of individuals and states that an organization will survive when the side payments of incentives it makes to the members who make up the coalition are in equilibrium with their contributions (Barnard, 1937).

In a corporate organization, this coalition includes stakeholders such as management, employees, shareholders, suppliers, customers (consumers), and tax collectors (national and local governments) (Cyert and March, 1963, p. 27; Urabe, 1965, 1966, 1968; Monden, 1968).

The demand for side payments of incentives is a demand to satisfy the personal motivations of the individuals participating in the organization; when organizational equilibrium is expressed as an equation, it must satisfy the following relationships (Urabe, 1965):

$$Each\ member's\ contribution\ amount$$
$$\leqq incentive\ payment\ amount\ to\ that\ member. \tag{1}$$

Here, "each member's contribution amount" is the amount the member demands and the "added value that each member would earn acting alone (when not participating in the organization in question)." The actual incentive payment must not be lower than this demand amount. An organization survives once this balance is satisfactory to all stakeholders. If it is not, the organization will collapse. This unequal relationship is necessary to meet the demands of each member of an organization and to ensure the organization's survival. It is thus the social responsibility of the manager, who must adjust the balance.

Thus, "organizational equilibrium" is achieved when the above formula is satisfied — when each member is paid an incentive that meets, or is at least not below, their demand level.

Even given the trend for a balance similar to a traditional "market price balance," to be reached over the long term between the demand and the side payment, data on these price factors over the short term are unreliable, and the demand and supply (payment) may not balance (Cyert and March, 1963, p. 36).

The standard for individual's participation decision while an organization distributes incentives to each participant and thus survives is what Barnard refers to as the principle of "organizational 'efficiency'." This is the degree at which individual demands are satisfied.

4.2 Application of Barnard's organizational equilibrium theory to the "burden of compensation funds" and the "burden of turnaround funds"

4.2.1 Relationship between Barnard's organizational equilibrium theory and the condition of "individual rationality" in cooperative game theory

Barnard's Organizational Equilibrium Theory holds that an organization will survive when the following equation is satisfied:

$$\textit{Each stakeholder's contributions}$$
$$\leqq \textit{side payment of incentive to each stakeholder.} \qquad (1')$$

For corporate organizations, this relationship can be expressed as follows:

$$\textit{The amount of added value earned by a particular member acting alone}$$
$$\leqq \textit{the amount of incentive distributed to that particular member.}$$
$$(1'')$$

This equation is the same as the "individual rationality" condition in cooperative game theory, according to which guaranteeing a distributed benefit that exceeds the "benefit of a particular member acting alone" is necessary to motivate the member to participate in an organization.

In such cases, the cooperative game theory standard for distributing the "joint benefit earned by the grand coalition (i.e., entire organization)" is a distribution in proportion to the "earned benefit of a particular member acting alone," where there is no *partial coalition* between several members.

Applying this distribution approach to Barnard's Organizational Equilibrium Model would result in an allocation of the organization's incentive financial resources in proportion to the contribution of each member.

In this application of game theory, the allocation amount of incentive financial resources is determined by the following formula:

$$\textit{Distribution amount } \phi i \textit{ of incentive financial resources to member } i$$
$$= \Big\{ \textit{contribution amount of member } i \textit{ acting alone } Ri$$
$$\div \Big(\textit{sum of all members' contribution amounts of acting alone} \sum Ri \Big) \Big\}$$
$$\times \textit{organization's total incentive financial resources } R_N. \qquad (2)$$

Here $\{Ri / \sum Ri\}$ in the above equation is the fair rate of contribution by the member i. The "organization's total incentive financial resources R_N"

is also the "joint contribution amount obtained through the collaborative action of all members in the organization." In other words, R_N is the total added value earned by the grand coalition.

Therefore,

$$\phi i = \left(Ri \div \sum Ri \right) \times R_N \tag{2'}$$

$$= Ri + \left(Ri \div \sum Ri \right) \times \left(R_N - \sum Ri \right). \tag{3}$$

The relationship $(R_N > \sum Ri)$ occurs due to the synergy effect generated by the grand coalition. This relationship also holds when the figures of Eq. (1″) summed for all members of the organization. Equation (3) is the so-called "Moriarity's Allocation Formula" (Moriarity, 1975) and satisfies the "individual rationality" condition $(\phi i > Ri)$ and the "group rationality" condition $(\sum \phi i = R_N)$ of cooperative game theory (Shubik, 1962).

We now examine how the "contribution amount of member i acting alone" of Eq. (2′) might be measured in the case of a nuclear power company such as TEPCO. One way would be to find a company in the same industry that has achieved average (or minimum) profitability and measure the *added value* on total revenue obtained by each member of the company. Thus, a regionally monopolistic Japanese electric power company that has achieved an average level of profitability can be examined, and the added value on total revenue to each stakeholder can be measured through a compositional breakdown of the company's "full cost" by each cost item (see the income statement of Fig. 2 for identifying each cost item).

Such item cost ratio on total revenue (= amount of each cost item ÷ total revenue) multiplied by the TEPCO' total revenue will be Ri of member i. These amounts Ri will represent the desired amount of return (i.e., opportunity cost) that TEPCO's stakeholders demand from TEPCO.

4.2.2 *"Side payment of negative incentives" for "negative contributions" of organization members: Fair distribution of burden among organization members*

The foregoing has examined the problem of members' positive contribution to an organization. However, the stakeholders of an organization that has caused a nuclear accident have made a negative contribution to the organization:

Investors: The investors in a company that has caused a nuclear accident have failed to exercise proper governance over that company.

Government: The government, representing citizens, has neglected to supervise the company.

Consumers: Consumers supported the policymakers (Diet members) who promoted the hazardous nuclear power generation program and the company that operated it. Moreover, consumers were attracted by the initial promise of cost efficiency, since electric power appears superficially cheap, and failed to notice that the true cost (mostly "Social Costs" of Kapp (1950)) of nuclear power generation is actually very high.

Local residents and local governments: Local residents and governments accepted subsidies (nuisance money) in return for accepting the building of the nuclear power plant.

Employees: Employees were satisfied to be employed by a nuclear power company that did not take sufficient care of safety. Moreover, as employees, they did not maintain safety while operating the power station.

Management: Management was consigned to operate the nuclear power company based on the government's nuclear power policy. However, management did not perform its agency, or fiduciary, responsibilities, especially that of ensuring safety.

Each stakeholder of the nuclear power company must accept a "fair portion of the burden of compensation funds" and a "fair portion of the burden of restructuring funds" in light of the loss (the negative contribution) based on the stakeholders' errors, or rebuilding society fairly will be difficult. These "burdens" are the "side payments of negative incentives."

Expressing this as an equation would yield the following:

$$\text{Minus contribution from each member acting alone}$$
$$\leqq \text{Minus incentive paid to each member.} \qquad (4)$$

If the "minus" is removed from this equation, the direction of the inequality sign will be reversed. Exchanging the minus contribution in this equation for "attributed loss" and the minus incentive for "allocated burden" would yield the following relationship:

$$\text{Loss amount attributed by each member acting alone}$$
$$\geqq \text{Burden allocated to each member.} \qquad (4')$$

The "loss amount attributed by each member acting alone" can be defined as the "amount of the cost item attributed by each stakeholder acting alone." Note that in this definition in Eq. (4'), we regard the "amount of the cost item" as the *loss amount*, while we regarded the same "amount of the cost item" as the *contribution amount* in Eq. (2).

The attributed cost of each member occupied in the total expenses in the income statement of the electric power company with average profitability is regarded as the "*added value*" yielded by each stakeholder acting alone, but on the other hand, it is considered by the company as the consumed resource amount or the "*sacrificed value*" caused by each stakeholder acting alone.

Further, the item cost ratio on total revenue (= amount of each cost item ÷ total revenue) of the electric power company of average profitability, multiplied by the TEPCO' total revenue, will yield the "loss amount attributed by each member acting alone."

Now the "burden allocation amount for each member" can be calculated, when there are no *partial coalitions* (i.e., partial coalitions among several members), by applying Eq. (2) as follows:

Burden allocation amount mi for member i

$$= \left\{ loss\ amount\ from\ member\ i\ acting\ alone\ Yi \right.$$

$$\left. \div \left(sum\ of\ loss\ amounts\ from\ all\ members\ acting\ alone \sum Yi \right) \right\}$$

$$\times\ total\ required\ incentive\ financial\ resources\ of\ the\ organization\ Y_N$$

$$\tag{5}$$

$$mi = \left(Yi \div \sum Yi \right) \times Y_N \tag{5'}$$

$$= Yi - \left(Yi \div \sum Yi \right) \times \left(\sum Yi - Y_N \right). \tag{6}$$

These equations are also the Moriarity's Allocation Formula (Moriarity, 1975), and, as with Eqs. (2) and (3), they satisfy the "individual rationality" condition ($mi < Y_i$) and the "group rationality" condition ($\sum mi = Y_N$) of cooperative game theory.

The "total required incentive financial resources of the organization Y_N" on the right side of Eq. (5') represents the total financial resources required to restructure a nuclear power company, while the liability for damages assigned to a nuclear power company comprises the total financial resources required for that liability — in other words, the envisaged total loss amount: financial resources are ultimately "funds."

The Y_N can be measured by the following method:

As stated in Sec. 3.1, making up the losses on TEPCO's income statement will require both a cost reduction and an expansion in sales revenues. This can be again expressed as follows:

$$\text{"Loss amount"} = \text{"Total required cost reduction amount"}$$
$$+ \text{"Sales revenue increase amount"}.$$

The top management's broad provisional standard for distributing the burden may be to apportion the current estimated loss based on a proportion between the current actual net sales amount and the current actual cost amount and then distribute this between a "burden on consumers (i.e., electricity price increases)" and a "burden on suppliers and employees and so forces to be allocated by internal functional divisions (i.e., target for the total cost reduction amount)."

The joint losses suffered by the nuclear power company as a whole Y_N will be lower than "the total loss amount $\sum Y_i$ of every member acting alone." That is $\sum Y_i > Y_N$, because Y_N is derived from the total loss in the TEPCO's income statement after the accident while $\sum Y_i$ is the "full costs" appeared in the income statement on the basis of item cost rate of the electric power company of average profitability. In addition, the members' collaboration creates a kind of synergy effect that reduces the company's total losses. Thus the amount of *reduced losses* $(\sum Y_i - Y_N)$ by the grand coalition will be allocated by Eq. (6) to the "loss amount attributed by each member acting alone" (Y_i).

Finally let the authors show the numerical example that clarifies Eq. (5′). For this purpose we assume:

Y_1 = material costs for the fuel procurement that might accrue if the *supplier* supplied the fuel to the other electric power company independently $= 10$.

Y_2 = labor costs if the *employee* worked at the other electric power company independently $= 6$.

Y_3 = costs of capital if the *investor* invested the funds to the other electric power company independently $= 4$.

Thus $\sum Y_i = 10 + 6 + 4 = 20$.

In addition, assume that these figures were estimated based on the *cost rate on the sales revenue* of the average profitability company of the electric power industry, and each rate was multiplied by the sales revenue of TEPCO *before* the accident.

Further assume that:

Y_N = total required cost reduction amount of TEPCO *after* the disaster
   $= 14$.

Then applying Eq. (5′), the allocated burden of supplier, employee, and investor will be:

$$mi = \left(Yi \div \sum Yi\right) \times Y_N$$
$$m_1 = (10/20)14 = 7$$
$$m_2 = (6/20)14 = 4.2$$
$$m_3 = (4/20)14 = 2.8.$$

The above computation implies that the total required cost reduction amount (Y_N) of TEPCO *after* the disaster will be distributed to each stakeholder in proportion to the "amount of the cost item attributed by each stakeholder acting alone (Yi)." Also since the total required cost reduction amount cannot be bigger than the sum of the cost item attributed by each stakeholder acting alone," the relationship of $(\sum Yi > Y_N)$ always holds.

Further, obviously the individual rationality $(m_i < Y_i)$ and the group rationality $(\sum m_i = Y_N)$ will also hold.

References

Barnard, C.I. (1937). *The Functions of the Executive*, Cambridge, Mass.: Harvard University Press.

Cyert, R.M. and March, J.M. (1963). *A Behavioral Theory of the Firm*, Englewood, NJ: Prentice-Hall.

Fukui, H. (2011). Issues Remaining with the Nuclear Damage Liability Act (Pt. II) Corporate Reorganization Act is the Reason Behind Unlimited Liability, *The Nikkei "Economic Seminar"*, July 13 (in Japanese).

Kapp, K.W. (1950). *The Social Costs of Private Enterprise*, Cambridge, Mass.: Harvard University Press.

Kikkawa, T. (2012). Issues for Reorganization of TEPCO (Pt. I): Urgent Need to Renew Management Structure, *The Nikkei "Economic Seminar"*, May 9 (in Japanese).

Monden, Y. (1968). Organization Theory Structure for a Corporate Decision-Making Model, *Keiei Kaikei Kenkyu* [Institute of Management & Accounting Research, Aichi University], 12, 21–33 (in Japanese).

Moriarity, S. (1975). Another approach to allocating joint costs, *The Accounting Review*, 50(4), 791–795.

Morita, A. (2011). Issues Remaining with the Nuclear Damage Liability Law (Pt. I) Assuming Limited Operator Liability, *The Nikkei "Economic Seminar,"* July 12 (in Japanese).

Nakayama, A. (2012). Corporate Reorganization and Government Involvement 1), 2), 3), 4), 5), *The Nikkei "Comments on Current Topics,"* March 1–16 (in Japanese).

Nomura, S. (2011). Overview of Public Management of TEPCO (Pt. I) Questions over the Consistency of the Compensation Scheme, *The Nikkei "Economic Seminar,"* May 26.

Oshima, K. (2011). *Cost of Nuclear Power: Viewpoint for Energy Change*, Tokyo: Iwanami Shoten (in Japanese).

Saito, M. (2011). *The Economics of the Nuclear Crisis*, Tokyo: Nihon Hyouronsha.

Shubik, M. (1962). Incentives, decentralized control, the assignment of joint costs and internal pricing, *Management Science*, 8, 325–343.

The Nikkei (2011). Nuclear Damage Compensation Assistance Scheme to be Initiated, July 29 (in Japanese).

The Nikkei (2011). The Nuclear Damage Liability Facilitation Fund Act Passed, August 3 (in Japanese).

The Nikkei (2011). Reason for Avoiding TEPCO Insolvency, August 11 (in Japanese).

The Nikkei (2012). Nuclear Power Station Insurance Premiums 81.5 Billion Yen: 11. Companies Agree on TEPCO Compensation Payment Scheme, March 2 (in Japanese).

The Nikkei (2012). TEPCO to Use "Resona-Style" Nationalization and Capital Injection Before Bankruptcy, April 28 (in Japanese).

The Nikkei (2012). Additional Capital Injection of 1.07 Trillion, April 28 (in Japanese).

The Nikkei (2012). Outline of TEPCO's Comprehensive Business Plan, May 10 (in Japanese).

The Nikkei (2012). Impact of Preferred Shares on Shareholders? May 22 (in Japanese).

The Nikkei (2012). TEPCO to Increase Prices by 8.47% in September, July 19 (in Japanese).

The Nikkei (2012). TEPCO Price Increase 8.46%, July 25 (in Japanese).

The Nikkei (2012). Seven Strategies for Restructuring TEPCO, July 30 (in Japanese).

The Nikkei (2012). Nationalization of TEPCO Complete, July 31 (in Japanese).

The Nikkei (2012). TEPCO to be Nationalized to Cope with Dire Problems, August 1 (in Japanese).

The Nikkei (2012). Japan Airlines and the Power of Legal Bankruptcy: Shares to Be Listed After 2 Years and 7 Months, September 20 (in Japanese).

Urabe, K. (1965). Critical examination of the Barnard-Simon Organizational Equilibrium Theory, *Kokumin Keizai Zasshi*, 111(2), 36–55 (in Japanese).

Urabe, K. (1966). *Developments of Modern Management Theory*, Tokyo: Yuhikaku Publishing Co., Ltd. (in Japanese).

Urabe, K. (ed.) (1968). *Corporate Behavioral Science*, Tokyo: Kajima Institute Publishing Co., Ltd. (in Japanese).

Yamauchi, H. (2011). Overview of Public Management of TEPCO (Pt. II): Supply Structure Reviewed after Recovery, *The Nikkei "Economic Seminar,"* May 25 (in Japanese).

Supplementary Reference Resources

The Nuclear Damage Liability Facilitation Fund Act, August 10, 2011, Act No. 94. (in Japanese).

Nuclear Damage Liability Facilitation Fund and Tokyo Electric Power Company, Incorporated (2012). *Comprehensive Special Business Plan*, April 27. Available at: http://www.meti.go.jp/press/2012/05/20120509010/20120509010-3.pdf. Accessed July 27, 2012 (in Japanese).

The Federation of Electric Power Companies of Japan. Available at: http://www.fepc.or.jp/enterprise/ryokin/index.html. Accessed July 28, 2012 (in Japanese).

The Act on Compensation for Nuclear Damage, June 17, 1961, Act. No. 147 (in Japanese).

proceedings be implemented in order to stop its mandatory payments to banks and financial institutions. This process of resolving disputes falls outside of the normal judicial process in Japan (METI, 2010). It was expected to take time for ETIC to make a decision in support of JAL because of the need for due diligence. Given this, the DBJ provided JAL with a bridge loan of 55 billion yen in November and December 2009 and 45 billion yen in January 2010 in order to support the company's business (Katayama and Kawamoto, 2011).

When the government decided not to guarantee the loans of the DBJ or legislate the act on special measures to sustain the company's operations, JAL's stock price further declined. Finally, ETIC guaranteed the DBJ's loans in order to stabilize the situation (Oshika, 2010). To maintain the continued operations of Japan Airlines, a control room was established in the company's headquarters to support financing, airline operations, revenue management, and communications. Fifty lawyers were stationed at airports in 22 countries to facilitate the transactions of affiliated companies that had not filed petitions for court protection with Japan Airlines Co., Ltd., and two other subsidiaries. Furthermore, some countries did not automatically permit the company's bankruptcy court protection when the relevant petition was filed in Japan. For example, in the United States, a separate petition had to be filed for this purpose (*The Nikkei*, 2010b). In China, JAL staff members had to explicitly explain that they would not have any problems making prompt payments for trade claims (*Shukan Diamond*, 2012a).

5 Background of Bankruptcy Proceedings

As mentioned in Sec. 4, the new Corporate Rehabilitation Law and resulting court procedure in the Tokyo District Court allowed for the preservation of trade claims and possession by debtors. If this new legal scheme had not been implemented, it might have been difficult for JAL to continue running its operations smoothly throughout its bankruptcy proceedings. *The Nikkei* (2010a), quoting the views of Hideo Seto, an ETIC trustee, argues that the JAL bankruptcy proceedings were indispensable to sorting out the entangled interests of the company's stakeholders, which included more than 400,000 shareholders, competing labor unions, and retired employees who disagreed with the reduction in pension payments. In addition to these entangled interests, the company's financial statements involved hidden costs. The first case of this was connected to the company's accounting practices in purchasing aircraft. JAL recorded its purchases from manufacturers but also recorded the sales of aircraft to a lease company. JAL described this as a capital gain in so-called "credit memos," which were profit notices from the vendors of the aircraft. With these paper gains, the company boosted its bottom line from fiscal 2002 through 2004 (Compliance Investigation Committee, 2010).

The second such case involved impairment accounting of aircraft. JAL categorized its entire fleet as one asset group for impairment accounting purposes. As a result, it did not recognize impairments in individual aircraft unless cash flows from operating activities were negative for the fiscal year in question (Compliance Investigation Committee, 2010). Even if the fair value of individual aircraft fell, the book value of these aircraft was not decreased as long as operating cash flows were positive. Hatakeyama (2010) indicated that losses based on the reevaluation of old aircraft were expected to come to more than 110 billion yen, based on the due diligence of the government task force and ETIC.

The third case involved losses accrued through hedging on fuel oil. JAL engaged in swap transactions for North Crude, a kind of crude oil. Between July and September 2008, during a peak in crude oil price, the company increased the hedge ratio, raising its position betting on further increases in the oil price. Later in 2008, the price of crude oil declined and the company suffered from hedge losses (Compliance Investigation Committee, 2010). According to the company's securities report, which is the equivalent of the American Form 10-K, its balance sheet showed deferred hedge losses of 201.8 billion yen at the end of March 2009.

These hidden costs in JAL's balance sheets made it quite difficult to restructure the business without court protection in its bankruptcy proceedings.

6 Reorganization Plan

The Tokyo District Court passed a reorganization plan for JAL and two of its subsidiaries on November 30, 2010. The major focuses of the business plan were as follows:

(1) JAL planned to reduce the number of types of aircraft that it operated, in order to increase efficiency. The Boeing 747-400, Airbus A300-600, McDonnell Douglas MD-81, and MD-90 were scheduled to retire earlier than originally planned.

JAL used to operate too many types of aircraft. By contrast, Southwest Airlines, the predecessor of successful modern low-cost carriers, used only one type of aircraft, the Boeing Co. 737. Operating only certain types of aircraft increases efficiency, because each type of plane needs a licensed pilot and aircraft maintenance crew that is specifically trained for that type (Ono, 2010).

The Boeing Co. 747-400 has a large passenger capacity and is useful during high seasons, but had too much capacity for JAL's low seasons. The company had to sell tickets at a discount in off-peak seasons.

(2) JAL planned to employ smaller aircraft, introducing the Boeing 737-800, Model E170 Regional Jet, and Boeing 787 on its international routes.

Frequent service with smaller aircraft allowed JAL to increase its market share (Ono, 2010), which was essential for improving the profitability of its business.

(3) JAL planned to cut unprofitable routes.

It was not easy for the company to determine which routes to withdraw, but it decided to do so by considering the fixed costs involved in supporting terminals. If one route from a terminal was not profitable and the profits of its other routes did not cover the terminal's fixed costs, the company shut down the terminal (*Shukan Diamond*, 2012c).

(4) JAL planned to reform the remuneration and fringe benefits system for employees.

In the past, JAL had not taken the performance of each employee into account in the employee's remuneration. It determined that offering incentives would increase employee performance. Compared to competing firms, the past fringe benefits such as pension payment for JAL directors and employees were also considered extravagant.

(5) JAL planned to sell and shut down subsidiaries and affiliates.

The company planned to sell subsidiaries and affiliates whose business operations did not offer potential for synergy with the airline industry. Its intention was to concentrate its resources on its core business.

(6) JAL planned to reduce its workforce through the enforcement of early retirement and the sale of subsidiaries. It planned to slash its number

of employees from 48,714 at the end of March 2010 to 32,600 at the end of March 2011.

The company reduced its domestic and international routes as a part of restructuring. It also downsized its fleet. As such, it had to reduce the size of its workforce in order to lower and regain profitability.

(7) JAL attempted to optimize its domestic and international routes.

In the domestic market, the company planned to increase the frequency of service while employing smaller aircraft. In international markets, the company planned to concentrate on servicing major European and American routes as well as rapidly growing Asian routes.

(8) In terms of its cargo business, JAL planned to concentrate on services employing the belly cargo space of its passenger aircraft, while suspending the operation of freighters.

(9) The company planned to simplify its management organization to increase efficiency. It also intended to create a department responsible for analyzing the profitability of each of the international and domestic routes.

At the time when the reorganization plan was developed, several of JAL's departments were redundant or had overlapping functions. Under the plan, each department and route was made responsible for its own profitability. The Managing Division, Route Marketing, was set up to calculate the profitability of each route, calculating profits as revenue minus the transferred price of crew and aircraft from other departments.

(10) The company planned to take advantage of the resources of its alliance partners. It intended to file for antitrust immunity for its alliance with American Airlines, with the aim of launching a joint enterprise.

(11) The company planned to efficiently share business policies and strategies with its subsidiaries and affiliates. It also established an effective management control system for clarifying the profit responsibilities of each subsidiary or affiliate company. JAL planned to more promptly collect financial data as well.

(12) The company aimed to manage the costs of maintaining airport facilities. The measures included the review of operational needs for office space and of the partial returns of terminal buildings as well as negotiations to lower the rent for shared space with other airlines. The company also reduced its workforce and outsourcing expenses.

(13) JAL planned to renovate its information system, which had been launched more than 30 years earlier. It intended to increase the efficiency and functionality of the system and decrease the associated maintenance costs.

(14) As taxes on fuel oil and landing fees required the spending of more than 10% of the company's revenue on international and domestic routes, JAL intended to request that these burdens be reduced, in order to improve its bottom line.

Even before filing for bankruptcy protection, JAL had considered employing smaller aircraft to increase efficiency and profitability. The major obstacle preventing this was that the company would have had to absorb huge losses in the sale of obsolete aircraft, which would wipe out its capital. Under bankruptcy protection, JAL could relinquish its capital, while fundamental restructuring became more feasible based on the consensus of diverse stakeholders.

Japan Airlines did not have enough assets whose fair value was higher than their book value, and thus, could not avoid insolvency by recognizing gains in asset sales, meaning that the company needed court protection. In this sense, the revitalization of JAL was different from that of other companies, such as Nissan Motor.

7 Stakeholder Burdens

Japan Airlines had net revenue of 1,204.8 billion yen in the fiscal year 2011. Its operating income was 204.9 billion yen for the same period. The company's passenger load factor jumped from 61.1% in the first quarter of fiscal 2011 to 73.4% in the first quarter of fiscal 2012. However, the improvement in the company's financial performance was achieved through the burdens of stakeholders such as capital reduction and downsizing.

In this section, the burdens of individual stakeholders involved in the restructuring of Japan Airlines are examined.

7.1 *Shareholders*

Under its reorganization plan, Japan Airlines International Co., Ltd., a subsidiary of Japan Airlines Co., Ltd., merged with Japan Airlines and JAL Capital Co., Ltd., a financial subsidiary. Japan Airlines International (JALI) continues to exist and has now been renamed Japan Airlines (JAL).

Existing shareholder equity was wiped out through a 100% capital reduction. JAL issued 350 billion yen in new shares to ETIC. The burden of the cost for existing shareholders was the whole amount of their investment.

7.2 *Banks and financial institutions*

Under JAL's reorganization plan, its creditors waived 87.5% of its general rehabilitation claim. MLIT (2012) indicates that the amount of waived debt in the fiscal year ending in March 2010 was 521.5 billion yen.

In reorganizations under the Corporate Rehabilitation Law, common benefit claims are prioritized for payment. Common benefit claims are claims for payment made for the benefit of all interested parties. They also include DIP financing and remuneration claims. According to MLIT (2012), at the end of March 2010, the DIP financing for JAL amounted to 360 billion yen, while the rest of the common benefit claim totaled 1,226.9 billion yen.

In reorganizations, claims secured by security interests are called rehabilitation security rights. Claims other than common benefit claims and rehabilitation security rights are called rehabilitation claims. They are unsecured debts which are not prioritized in the reorganization. In the case of Japan Airlines, the amount of rehabilitation claim was 595.6 billion yen (MLIT, 2012).

In the process of creating the reorganization plan for Japan Airlines, JAL and the banks engaged in serious negotiations regarding the number of routes that should be discontinued by the company. MLIT and some other banks insisted that all international routes be discontinued (*Shukan Diamond*, 2012b). DBJ and the bankruptcy trustees considered discontinuing more routes than had originally been planned under Plan C. In Plan C, domestic routes mostly served by a pre-merger airline, Japan Air System, would be discontinued and some pilots would be dismissed. Considering future competition with LCCs over short and mid-range routes, it was then determined that it would be practical for JAL to maintain its long-range international routes (Ono, 2010). The banks suffered tremendous losses in waiving debts but negotiated further restructuring to stop operating losses and improve the likelihood of a successful revitalization process.

After it filed for court protection, JAL's leased aircraft could have been seized or foreclosed on by its lessors or lenders to its lessors. As such, it was crucial that JAL make lease payments to the financial firms involved, in order to ensure the smooth operation of the company (Katayama and Kawamoto, 2011).

7.3   *Passengers and local airports*

MLIT (2012) states that JAL's domestic routes were reduced from 148 at the end of March 2010 to 109 at the end of March 2013, while international routes were reduced from 75 at the end of March 2010 to 65 at the end of March 2013. Compared to fiscal 2008, ASK (available seat kilometers) were reduced by roughly 30% for domestic routes and roughly 40% for international routes by the second half of fiscal 2010 (Japan Airlines, 2010). ASK is the measure of available seats multiplied by the distance of the flights involved.

JAL serves domestic routes flown by local inhabitants of Japan. A local subsidiary on a northern island, Hokkaido Air System (HAC), was partially owned by JAL in the past. HAC serves the Okadama airport in Sapporo and the Okushiri airport, located on a small island in the west of Hokkaido. By reducing its shareholding from 51% to 14.5%, JAL virtually withdrew from the local transportation market in Hokkaido. HAC faced accumulated losses of 210 million yen at the end of March 2010. After reducing its capital, new shares were issued to the governments of Hokkaido and Sapporo city (*The Nikkei*, 2010d). HAC issued 52 million yen in new shares to the Hokkaido government, which allocated 573 million yen for HAC's budget for the fiscal year ending in March 2012 (*The Nikkei*, 2011a).

In Nagoya, JAL planned to withdraw service from Komaki Airport, but the local communities fiercely opposed the termination of scheduled flights. Fuji Dream Airlines, an independent airline company, now provides service to existing routes from Komaki Airport (*The Nikkei*, 2010g).

JAL's withdrawals have left local communities and other airlines to bear the resulting costs.

7.4   *Employees*

According to data provided by Japan Airlines, remuneration to its pilots was reduced by 21% from fiscal 2008 to fiscal 2011. During the same period, remuneration was reduced by 24% for cabin attendants and 25% for ground staff. Pilots and cabin attendants were previously provided with guaranteed amounts of flight time by JAL. Cabin attendants had 50 hours of monthly guaranteed flight time. Pilots and co-pilots had guaranteed flight times of 65 hours and other fixed allowances. After the reorganization, all of the guaranteed flight times for cabin attendants were abolished, and they are paid by flight hourly wage. Moreover, while pilots and cabin crew were previously provided with taxis and hired cars as means of traveling to and from airports, they now have to use public transportation during operating hours (*The Nikkei*, 2010f).

Since the restructuring of JAL involved an injection of public funds, the lucrative pension payments offered to employees and directors of the company were heavily criticized in the mass media. Employee pension payments were then reduced by an average of roughly about 50% in response. Payments to retired employees were also cut by about 30% (*The Nikkei*, 2010c).

JAL faced conflicts with labor unions in undergoing reorganization. For example, the Tokyo Metropolitan Labor Relations Commission ordered the company to put a letter of apology on a bulletin board of the company. In November 2010, ETIC, JAL's bankruptcy trustee, threatened not to invest in JAL if two labor unions carried out strikes that they had proposed (*The Nikkei*, 2011b).

7.5 *Suppliers*

Under the reorganization plan, suppliers' trade claims were preserved. JAL made payments for trade claims after getting permission from the Tokyo District Court (Katayama and Kawamoto, 2011). This arrangement was necessary for the continued operation of the company, as it would have had to stop operations if its suppliers had refused to provide fuel and other supplies.

7.6 *Government-affiliated organizations*

JAL was in a dire financial situation in late 2009 and could not borrow money from private banks. Meanwhile, ETIC could not offer loans before making official decisions on financial support that involved due diligence. Thus, the DBJ provided a bridge loan of 100 billion yen to the company (Katayama and Kawamoto, 2011). This bridge loan was preserved as pre-DIP financing under JAL's reorganization plan, but in fiscal 2009, the DBJ experienced losses of 20 billion yen in preferred stocks that had been issued in March 2008 (*The Nikkei*, 2010e).

8 Amoeba Management[1]

Under the reorganization plan, Kazuo Inamori, founder and chairman emeritus of Kyocera Corporation, was invited to become the chairman of Japan Airlines. Inamori introduced the amoeba management system to the company.

Amoeba management has three pillars: (1) the amoeba organization, (2) the amoeba leader, (3) and the "hourly efficiency" management accounting system. An amoeba organization is a small accounting unit that is responsible for profitability but operates based on the principles of functional management. In the amoeba accounting system, added value is calculated as subtracting deductions from unit revenue. In this calculation system, labor expenses are not included in deductions. Thus, amoeba leaders do not have incentives to cut labor costs for increasing profits. Instead, added value is divided by total working hours, and the resulting quotient is called "hourly efficiency." "Hourly profit" is then calculated by subtracting hourly wages from "hourly efficiency." The amoeba leader tries to increase revenue and decrease costs in the business unit while flexibly responding to changes in the business environment. The amoeba leader also tries to decrease the organization's total working hours. Amoeba organizations try to avoid opportunity loss and achieve profit maximization through profit chain management (Kazusa, 2007; Inamori, 2012).

In Japan Airlines, the basic unit of the divisional accounting system is based on the individual route and flight. The Managing Division, Route Marketing, has been set up to analyze the cost and revenue of each flight. This department is a kind of profit controller, which leases aircraft, cabin attendants, pilots, and maintenance crew from other departments and sets the public fare for each individual flight utilizing the revenue management system to maximize its revenue. It then realizes the profits of each flight as the difference between revenue and lease costs. If the price of the public fare falls due to market conditions, the department requests lower costs of resources from departments that provide the services. For example, the Department of Cabin Attendants can decrease locker space and cut expenditures on photocopies and electricity to lower costs or increase in-flight sales, thus boosting its own profitability (*Shukan Diamond*, 2012a).

Amoeba management allows for quick responses to market changes. For example, after the Tohoku earthquake of 2011, JAL provided special flights in the Tohoku area and transferred large aircraft to the region, responding to demand in the area damaged by the earthquake (*Shukan Diamond*, 2012a). These kinds of efforts also motivate employees to increase their efficiency and continuously improve the business.

In the original amoeba management system within Kyocera, the "Kyocera Philosophy" played an important role. This philosophy involved a set of plain sentences about life and management.

After introducing the amoeba management system, Japan Airlines developed its own philosophy, called JAL philosophy. Some aspects have been taken from the Kyocera Philosophy, but most have been created by the company's own employees. In the amoeba management system, each amoeba, or division, pursues its own profits, which might lead to the pursuit of self-interested goals or even conflicts between different divisions. JAL philosophy prevents this by establishing a sense of teamwork through shared objectives and behavioral standards. JAL employees are periodically required to attend training sessions on JAL philosophy. In these training sessions, employees discuss important issues within the company and share their knowledge with other departments. This has kept morale in the company high even after its drastic restructuring.

9   Concluding Remarks

In the restructuring and revitalization of Japan Airlines, the Japanese government and government-affiliated organizations have played significant roles. The Development Bank of Japan provided a vital bridge loan before the company filed for bankruptcy protection and an injection of public funds during its financial crisis. Enterprise Turnaround Initiative Corporation took strong initiative in turning JAL around. Tomiyama (2012) argues that the injection of public funds was justified in this case, because of the company's cash shortages, immediate need of equity investment, and its vital role in the Japanese economy.

In terms of legal factors, the new corporate rehabilitation law and the support of Tokyo District Court was essential to JAL's continued operation. A debt waiver and drastic restructuring allowed the company to turn itself around and succeed beyond expectations. New management helped Japan Airlines work through its revitalization process with the amoeba management system, which helped to keep employees market-oriented and maintained morale in a difficult business environment.

It is important to make sound policy judgments in order to maintain fair levels of competition in the wake of this government intervention into the airline industry. At the same time, it is crucial to engage in solid policy planning, determining how and to what extent the government should play a role in the field of public transportation in a period of slow economic growth and difficult budgetary situations.

End Note

1. We interviewed Mr. Masamitsu Mizonoue, Vice President, Public Relations, and Mr. Naoya Yoshida, Assistant Manager, Planning Group, Public Relations of Japan Airlines Co., Ltd. in August 2012.

References

Compliance Investigation Committee (2010). Investigative Report. August 26 (in Japanese).

Hatakeyama, H. (2010). Rehabilitation issue of JAL, *Rippo To Chosa,* February, pp. 169–178 (in Japanese).

Inamori, K. (2012). About Amoeba Management, Kazuo Inamori Official Web Site. Available at: http://global.kyocera.com/inamori/management/amoeba/index.html. Accessed September 14, 2012.

Japan Airlines (2010). JAL Group News, April 28.

Katayama, E. and Kawamoto, S. (2011). Business Revitalization Process of Japan Airlines, *Jigyo Saisei To Saiken Kanri.* July 5, pp. 152–165 (in Japanese).

Kazusa, Y. (2007). Big Family Management of Kyocera and Management Accounting, *Journal of Management Accounting,* 15(2), pp. 3–17 (in Japanese).

Ministry of Economy, Trade and Industry (2010). Turnaround ADR (Alternative Dispute Resolution). January (in Japanese).

Ministry of Land, Infrastructure, Transport and Tourism (2012). Recent Trend in Airline Industry. July 19 (in Japanese).

Mori, I. (2010) *Kusatta Tsubasa (Rotten Wing),* Tokyo: Gentousha (in Japanese).

Namba, K., Watabe, Y., Suzuki, K. and Tokuoka, O. (2008). Recent Trend and New Practice in Corporate Rehabilitation, *Kinyu Homu Jijyo,* December 15, pp. 24–39 (in Japanese).

Ono, N. (2010) *Kyozo No Hyouryuu,* Tokyo: Koudansha (in Japanese).

Oshika, Y. (2010). *Ochita Tsubasa.* Tokyo: Asahishinbun Shuppan (in Japanese).

Shukan Diamond (2012a). JAL Struggle to Revitalize Part 4, February 24 (in Japanese).

Shukan Diamond (2012b). JAL Opposes to Withdrawal of International Routes, April 12 (in Japanese).

Shukan Diamond (2012c). Feature Article Japan Airlines, Part 1, June 6 (in Japanese).

Takagi, S. (2006)*Jigyo Saisei (Business Revitalization)*, Tokyo: Iwanami Shoten (in Japanese).

The Nikkei (2010a). Restart of JAL with Prepackaged deal, January 20, p. 4 (in Japanese).

The Nikkei (2010b). Corporate Rehabilitation of JAL with Prepackaged Bankruptcy, February 1, 16 (in Japanese).

The Nikkei (2010c). Reduction of JAL Pension Payment Approved by MHLW. March 18, p. 9 (in Japanese).

The Nikkei (2010d). HAC, Issuing Stocks of 300 Million yen to Hokkaido, March 31, p. 1 (in Japanese).

The Nikkei (2010e). DBJ Made Profits after Recognizing Losses in Preferred Stocks of JAL, May 27, p. 4 (in Japanese).

The Nikkei (2010f). Pay cut of JAL, June 9, p. 12 (in Japanese).

The Nikkei (2010g). Survival of Local Airports after the Withdrawal of JAL, September 6, p. 29 (in Japanese)

The Nikkei. (2011a). Hokkaido Budgeted 600 Million yen to Support HAC, February 19, p. 1 (in Japanese).

The Nikkei (2011b). Tokyo Metropolitan Labor Relations Commission Recognized the Unlawful Intervention of ETIC in JAL union strikes, August 3, p. 14 (in Japanese).

Tomiyama, K. (2012). Corporate Revitalization with Government Support, part 1, *The Nikkei,* March 22, p. 31 (in Japanese).

PART 2

Private Turnaround to Cope with the Business Crisis

3

The Choice that Samsung Electronics Made in the Monetary Crisis of 1997

Hyeun Kyoung Song
Dongyang Mirae University

Gunyung Lee
Niigata University

1 Introduction

After spending 40 years attempting to learn from the strong points and technological competencies of existing companies in advanced countries, Samsung Electronics Co., Ltd., reached such a high standard that it is now positioned as a globally competitive technology company in the electronics industry. This can be seen from the fact that it holds the greatest share of global markets for different products, including TVs, semiconductors, LCDs (liquid crystal displays), and mobile phones.

Despite the fact that Samsung Electronics is now a leading company in the electronics industry, it has often been under pressure in the past, whether as a result of the International Monetary Fund (IMF) monetary crisis in late 1990s or the global economic crisis of the late 2000s. These unfortunate incidents have not only heavily affected Samsung Electronics but also led other Korean companies into bankruptcy. The incident where Korea asked IMF for a relief fund and entered under the management of IMF when the Korean economy was confronted bankruptcy is called the "IMF monetary crisis." During this crisis, the Samsung group had to reduce its number of affiliate companies from 140 to 83 and downsize its workforce from 160,000 to 115,000 workers, in order to accomplish an extreme structural readjustment (Hatamura and Yoshikawa, 2009, pp. 62–68).

This chapter will focus on how Samsung Electronics managed to overcome its difficulties and explain the strategic decisions that the company made during the "analog to digital" paradigm shift period accompanying IT innovation. In particular, the leadership perspective of Kunhee Lee, the chairman of Samsung Electronics, will be discussed, along with the following four types of management strategies:

1. Management by discarding: Selecting business areas that would allow the company to overcome the IMF monetary crisis.
2. Management by focusing on quality: Establishing the foundation to restructure the business after the IMF monetary crisis.
3. Management by balancing: Building a business portfolio for crisis management.
4. Self-controlling management: Decision-making mechanism to manage uncertainty.

2   The Past and Future of Samsung Electronics[1]

Although by 2011, Samsung Electronics had become a global company with 897.5 billion won in capital and 101,970 employees, it had initially started as a small industrial company founded in 1969. At that time, it had only 330 million won in capital and 36 employees. The company has made a dramatic transition from an electronics company that relied only on the domestic Korean market to a global export company. This section provides an overview of how Samsung made it to the top of the global market for TVs, semiconductors, LCDs, and mobile phones, including smart-phones.

The story of Samsung's TV business started in 1975, when the company began producing the Econo TV, an electrical power-saving TV constructed by applying the Quick Start Braun Tube method. This TV model opened up a new path for the company, creating a sensation and causing Samsung to become the leading TV company in terms of domestic market share as well as the world's foremost monochrome TV company. By 1992, the company was ranked second after Philips in terms of its share of the global TV market, holding a 6% share. While Sony was still working with Braun Tube TVs during the "analog to digital" paradigm shift period, Samsung Electronics was investing in LCD TVs. Finally, the developing of the Bordeaux TV in 2006 gave Samsung Electronics the chance to overtake Sony, and it became the top-ranked TV company in the world in terms of global TV market share, although Sony had dominated the TV market for more than 30 years. For six years, from 2006 to 2011, Samsung Electronics held its position in the global TV market, and the company is now continuing its dominance as it releases new products, such as smart TVs and OLED TVs.

In 1974, Samsung Electronics purchased Korea Semiconductor and entered the semiconductor market. Although semiconductors are a technology-intensive product and the barrier to entering the field is thus high, semiconductor production holds high value-added potential. Because American and Japanese companies already possessed greatly advanced technologies at the time, Samsung was left behind for 13 years. Despite facing a deficit in its semiconductor business during this period, the company continued investing in the field and finally moved into the black in 1988. When Samsung Electronics first entered the semiconductor industry, its technology was said to be 30 years behind, compared to that of companies in advanced countries. However, 12 years later, the company had narrowed its technological lag to only two or three years. In 1992, by developing the world's first 64M DRAM (dynamic random-access memory), Samsung Electronics was able to gain the largest global share in the DRAM market.

During the silicon cycle recession, Samsung Electronics chose to invest actively. The company made this choice despite the investment risks involved because it felt that capital recovery and the first-mover advantage could be achieved by reducing new investment costs and supplying new products before rival companies and then selling these products at a high price when the economy recovers (Mitarai, 2005). Through this strategy, the company succeeded in the semiconductor business and expanded its overall domain. The manufacturing process of LCDs is similar to that of DRAM, and in the 1990s, Samsung began using LCDs in notebook PCs, desktop monitors, and mobile phones. Since the 2000s, it started integrating LCDs into TV displays, which is a business area that continues to grow.

In the 1990s, Japanese companies were the leaders of LCD and semiconductor industries. However, Samsung Electronics was able to capitalize on the first-mover advantage in these industries by investing in a project involving enlargement of mother-glass for liquid crystal panels during a depression using crystal cycles (Mitarai, 2005). Based on this step, the company was able to start increasing its market share in 1996, becoming the leading LCD company in the world in 2001.

Mobile communication service was made available in Korea in 1984. At the time, the domestic mobile phone market was dominated by the U.S. company Motorola. In September 1988, Samsung Electronics stepped into the market, with its analog mobile phone, the SH-100. This product had a number of issues, including frequent breakdowns and defects, due to the company's lack of core technology and experience. In order to solve the fundamental problems with its initial models, Samsung targeted Motorola for benchmarking and analysis. As a consequence, it was able to reduce the size and weight of its phones and improve their sound quality. Its 100 g mobile phone, the SH-700, was released in October 1993, and it gained a good reputation with customers, eventually coming to rule over the domestic mobile phone market. In October 1994, the SH-770 was introduced as a brand called "Anycall," whose market share accounted for 51.5% of the domestic market by the following year. Not only was Samsung able to rank first in the Korean market, but it also became the second-ranked mobile phone company in the global market.

In 2007, the market entry of the iPhone caused a disaster in the global IT market. Samsung Electronics misjudged its ability to develop smart-phones, and thus, despite holding the second largest global share of the mobile phone market, it was left behind in the smart-phone market. After making several attempts to improve its offerings, through phones such as the Omnia and Galaxy A, the company managed to release the Galaxy S in 2010. According to *Forbes*, an American economics magazine, by the first quarter of 2012, Samsung Electronics had moved forward to hold the greatest global share in the mobile market, at 28.8%, having sold 41 million phones (*Korea Herald Business*, April 2, 2012).

3 Samsung Electronics' Business Management: Overcoming the IMF Monetary Crisis

After the dishonor of the Hanbo group in January 1997, 16 out of 30 major Korean company groups went out of business. Their bankruptcies also influenced the general Korean financial market, causing the failure of more than 10 banks. After the Asian currency crisis, which began in Thailand in July 1997, Korea officially applied for IMF relief in November 1997. Regardless of this, the domestic environment in the country became chaotic: foreign currency holdings required for returning overseas bonds hit rock bottom, stock prices fell sharply, and Korea's national credit rating fell from A1 to BAA2 (almost junk). Within one year after joining the Organization for Economic Cooperation and Development (OECD), Korea had to face the IMF monetary crisis, which had disastrous effects on the nation. Korean people expressed their opinions on the IMF at the time by describing its initials as standing for "I'M Foolish," "I'M Fired," or "I'M Fighting" (Son, 2011, pp. 267–273).

Like the rest of the country, the Samsung group could not avoid the chaos caused by the IMF crisis. At the time, Samsung Electronics had maximized its profits (net income was 94.4 billion won in 1994 and 250.5 billion won in 1995) and was making preparations for a shift from the largest company in Korea to a dominant global organization. Unfortunately, a poorly planned advance into the overseas markets resulted in inconsistency in the company's overseas departments, yielding a large-scale deficit. In addition, the bubble economy hangover from the thriving semiconductor industry also contributed to a general deterioration in management performance and financial structuring. Moreover, rather than having a keen awareness of the risks that the company faced, Samsung's officers and employees were living in the present, strongly affected by their opinions of the company's greatness, and even expected an economic recovery. In reality, the IMF monetary crisis forced Samsung to face its most challenging period since its foundation. The company was able to persevere, however, through the new management and innovation approaches adopted by Kunhee Lee, its chairman. Lee was well aware of the risks that the company faced, but regarded the IMF monetary crisis as an opportunity for a fresh start.

In the following sections, the five factors that contributed to Samsung Electronics' recovery from the IMF monetary crisis are discussed. These are "management by discarding," "management by focusing on quality," "management by balancing," "self-controlling management," and "ownership by Kunhee Lee."

3.1 *A choice to conquer a crisis: Management by discarding*

In 1998, the Samsung group announced an innovative business quality scheme that would allow it to overcome the IMF monetary crisis. This included scaling down the organization by 30%, reducing total cost for that year by 50%, reducing executives' salaries by 10%, and reducing the investment scale by 30%. Samsung started by executing stricter structural adjustments in its organization and human resources. In order to reorganize the business structure, the company divided its businesses into four categories, preparing a counter-plan for each. "Seed businesses" were business areas considered likely to succeed in the future with the current-level investment, including mobile communication systems, networking, and non-memory business. "Sapling businesses" were those that were expected to prosper in the future but which were not currently productive, such as digital TVs, personal digital assistant machines (PDAs), and TFT-LCDs (super-thin liquid crystal displays). "Fruit businesses" were those that led the growth of the company, but needed to be improved, such as large-size color TVs, monitors, notebook PCs, mobile phones, and memory. "Dead tree businesses" were those that needed to be boldly adjusted, including analog semiconductors (produced at the company's Buchun factory) and personal audio devices. The audio business was sold, and its facility was relocated (*Korea Economic Daily*, 2002, pp. 101–102).

Samsung then concentrated on its central businesses such as semiconductors, the electronic communication of information, and digital apparatuses, while weaker businesses were reconfigured. More specifically, 34 of 52 businesses were adjusted, and 42 low value-added businesses were outsourced. A total of 13 of 79 overseas businesses that represented an ill-planned advance into the overseas market were also closed or withdrawn (Compilation Committee of Samsung Electronics, 2010, p. 442). In addition, the workforce was reduced from 58,000 to 42,000 in 1998, which represented an almost 30% reduction. Through these actions, Samsung Electronics implemented strong structural adjustments for short-term survival.

At the same time, a restructuring of Samsung's financial structure was carried out. This focused on the reduction of unnecessary expenses. The contraction of loans and inventories and the company's "inventory turnover period," which had been 100 days in 1994, was cut down to 37 days in 1998, were the focal issues. The effect of this reduction, in terms of numerical value, was 1.6 trillion won. The receivables collection period, which had been 80 days in 1994, was shortened to 41 days in 1998, which led to a 1 trillion won reduction in expenses (Compilation Committee of Samsung Electronics, 2010, p. 442). Furthermore, by implementing "profit-and-loss" and "cash-flow" centered management, the company ensured that its financial structure was stable. The cash flow of each branch was reported to the company every day. As a consequence, in spite of being in the middle of the IMF monetary crisis, Samsung increased its sales volume, from 11.5 trillion won in 1994 to 26 trillion won by 1999, and its operating income, from 2.6 trillion won in 1994 to 4.48 trillion won by 1999. Its debt ratio, which had been 219.34% in 1994, was decreased to 85.35% by 1999. Samsung Electronics thus managed to make a profit during the IMF monetary crisis by engaging in successful structural rearrangement and business reorganization.

3.2 The basis of overcoming the IMF monetary crisis: Management by focusing on quality

In June 1993, Kunhee Lee announced, in a conference held in Frankfurt, that Samsung would shift its policy from one that was "quantity-centered" to one that was "quality-centered." Within the company, this came to be known as "The Declaration of Frankfurt." This declaration was based on the chairman's opinion that a "small profits and quick returns" strategy of selling low-quality products at a low price would not be accepted by the global market. The company's quality-centered management in the following period was based on "personal innovation," which involved changing one's way of thinking; "process innovation," which involved reforming processes; and "product innovation," which involved aiming for more innovative production approaches. These were called the 3PI activities (Hatamura and Yoshikawa, 2009, pp. 43–52).

Samsung felt that, in order to implement quality-centered management, personal innovation was the most important. The purpose of personal innovation was to change the nature of the company's corporate culture. As a device, the "7–4 system," which set working hours from 7 am to 4 pm, was implemented. The aim of this system was to improve the quality of duty and increase concentration by enabling workers to avoid the rush hour and shorten commuting time. The system also improved the quality of life for workers, as it allowed them to have more time for self-learning and language studies after work.

Samsung also expanded its human resource development facilities and reformed its education programs during this time, which played an important role in changing the employees' ways of thinking. Its existing education programs had primarily concerned general training, while the new approach integrated global strategies. The company's education facilities also enabled the development of local professionals who were prepared to enter the global market (Hatamura and Yoshikawa, 2009, pp. 80–90).

Samsung's process innovation began with building the Product Data Management system. This was an information system governing and unifying all company information, including in areas such as design and development, and was used to improve efficiency and reduce the operational time. The construction of the base of this system started in 1994, and it was completed in 1996 (Hatamura and Yoshikawa, 2009, pp. 112–118). Samsung Electronics tried to make the most of the digital era in carrying out strategy reforms.

Samsung's approach to product innovation was more challenging. In November 1994, the wireless telephone division had to promote the production of goods of poor quality, of which 18% were defective. Although the company claimed that its new management approach was quality-centered, it continued to release distribute defective mobile phones to the market.

In fact, in March 1995, approximately 2,000 workers wearing headbands gathered in an open space in the company's Gumi factory, holding a banner that said, "Quality is my Character and Pride." The workers burned 150,000 electronic items such as mobile phones, key-phones, wireless telephones, and fax machines, which were worth 50 billion won in total (Lee, 2010, p. 298). This made workers resolved to ensure that the Anycall mobile brand was of better quality, and as a consequence, Anycall became a global brand.

Instead of pursuing absolute quality like the Japanese companies, Samsung Electronics aimed for relative quality, as determined by customer needs, circumstance, price, timing, and failure rate. This philosophy can be seen in the company's approach to repairs. Samsung's quality control staff regularly patrols Seoul by car, carrying spare parts with them so that they can exchange broken parts within one hour of receiving a breakdown report. They are also willing to replace base machinery and motors, discarding old broken parts. Sometimes this method is criticized for overlooking the causes of breakdowns, but such criticism is made only from a manufacturing point of view, and the Korean end-users are typically less interested in accurately identifying the cause of a problem than they are in it being repaired within one hour (*The Nikkei*, March 16, 2010). This example clearly presents the difference in the definition of quality in the analog and digital period.

Kunhee Lee's "quality-centered" management, which eventually helped to make the company globally competitive, was not successful from the outset. The structural adjustment that had to be made after the IMF monetary crisis instilled a sense of danger in employees and changed their ways of thinking. In this context, the 3PI activities managed to function as an infrastructure (Hatamura and Yoshikawa, 2009, pp. 70–71).

3.3   *A business portfolio for crisis management: Management by balancing*

Samsung Electronics maintains a balance between its different business sectors, such as home electric appliances, the electronic communication of information, semiconductors, and computers. Based on its success in the LCD sector, Samsung expanded its business into the mobile phone market. Because the DRAM market was flourishing in 1994, the company earned roughly more than 3 trillion won in operating income from the semiconductor sector. However, a sudden drop in the price of 16M DRAM in 1996 turned the situation around, and this did not improve in 1997. When

Samsung Electronics faced its biggest crisis, experts advised it to focus on semiconductors, which were its main business, and give up its other businesses. However, the export of mobile phones, which began in 1997, helped the company make profits. Although its operating income from the semiconductor sector, which had been 6 trillion won in 2000, had shrunk sharply to 690 billion won by 2001, its earnings from the mobile phone and home electric appliances sectors balanced this out. By 2001, the company had come to hold the biggest share of the global LCD market. Jongyong Yun, Samsung Electronics' vice chairman at the time, explained that the company's business portfolio, in which other sectors made up for losses in the semiconductor business, had proven effective (*Korea Economic Daily*, 2002, p. 124).

In order to promote its business portfolio, the Samsung group, as a whole, employed a vertically integrated business structure. Through collaboration with overseas enterprises, the company promoted the vertical systematization of materializing, manufacturing, and sales of final products. Panasonic Corporation, which has an in-sourcing rate of 50%, states that the advantages of vertical systematization are that it: (1) maintains product price by preventing the leakage of core components, (2) reduces costs through the external sale of mass-produced components, and (3) allows design modification and new technology applications to be carried out easily, so that products are more simply sold to the global market (*The Nikkei*, July 27, 2006).

As can be seen in Fig. 1, Samsung Electronics is supported by associated companies that belong to the Samsung group, which allows it to produce diverse electronic products and unify its competitive abilities (*Money Today*, June 14, 2011).

For example, OLED panels are installed in products such as smartphones, tablet PCs, and OLED TVs, and this is supported by the vertical

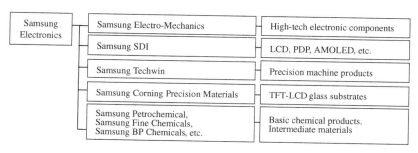

Fig. 1.   Vertical integration of Samsung Electronics.

systematization of a chain that involves Samsung Electronics (complete product), Samsung Display (panel), Cheil Industries (electronic materials), and Samsung Corning Advanced Glass (glass substrates) (*Etoday*, May 9, 2012).

3.4 A decision-making mechanism for managing uncertainty: Self-controlling management

Within Samsung Electronics, employees who are given authority are also expected to take responsibility. While the representatives of each of the company's business sectors are leading experts in their field, they are also held responsible for every decision that they make. Jonyong Yun, the company's vice chairman at that time, did so when he refused to accept the overseas investors' suggestion that the company should give up sectors other than semiconductors during the IMF monetary crisis. Yun felt that it was more important to look at future profitability than to give priority to present profitability. As a result, the mobile phone sector became a cash cow for the company, overtaking its semiconductor business.

When Samsung planned to invest a large amount of money into LCD production facilities in February 2002, Sangwan Lee, the president of the LCD sector, dogmatically made the decision to take responsibility for the entire initiative. It can also be said that Samsung Electronics' competitiveness comes from having a CEO who can say no to proposals and who takes full responsibility for the results of his decisions. This allows Samsung Electronics to predict future developments and make speedy decisions on present situations. The company does not resolve problems after they occur, but beforehand, and regularly discusses the potential problems and what to do when they occur. It is also willing to interrupt planned procedures and deal with environmental changes and unexpected market shifts (*Chosun Biz*, February 20, 2010).

Samsung also employs a differentiated compensation system based on performance and in correspondence to an employee's level of authority and responsibility. The compensation system of Samsung Electronics consists of three regimes: a profit-sharing system that adds rewards for group achievement, a productivity incentive system, and the annual salary system, which is based on individual performance. One special characteristic of Samsung's annual salary system, which was introduced in 1998, is that basic pay constitutes 60% of the total salary, while the remaining 40% is based on personal achievement. The profit-sharing system, which was introduced in 2000, is a compensation system that assesses performance and allots 20% of any achievement in excess of profit goals for distribution among employees. The productivity incentive system, which was instituted in 1992, was widely applied at the time when a fixed salary was used; this system evaluates the EVA (economic value-added), cash flow, and EPS (earnings per share) of each department, division, and the entire firm. Based on the results of this evaluation, an amount is paid to employees in addition to their base salaries (*Korea Economic Daily*, 2002, pp. 113–115).

3.5 *The axis of crisis control: Kunhee Lee's ownership*

One of the characteristics of Kunhee Lee is his insight into current developments. Lee became the second successor to the Samsung group in December 1987, and in the following year, which was the 50th anniversary of the company, he declared "the second establishment." In doing so, he emphasized the significance of change and reform in Samsung's future development into a world-class company. Nevertheless, it was not easy to change the company's tendency to see its own way as the best. Samsung Electronics was a relatively successful company. In May 1992, its color TV was chosen as a "world masterpiece"; it developed the world's first 64M DRAM; and its exports were worth over 4 billion dollars. Regardless of these achievements, Lee predicted a crisis in the company. The 1993 "Declaration of Frankfurt" was the biggest incident in the company. At that time, Samsung's overall organization was reformed, and the new management's approach was demonstrated by the famous slogan, "Change everything except for your wife and children!" While everyone else had been content with the state of the company, Lee felt impending danger and the need for reformation.

Lee's ownership has also been characterized by bold decision making. Though the semiconductor business is a risky one, requiring large initial investments of capital, Lee knew how valuable it was. For this reason, he purchased Korea Semiconductor with his own private funds before he became chairman, in spite of his father's opposition. This courageous investment was also made at a time when Japanese companies were facing a long-term recession. Lee's investments have kept Samsung's semiconductor sector at the top of the global market.

Another characteristic of Lee's ownership can be expressed by the slogan, "Don't employ him or her if suspicious, but if already started using him or her don't doubt." This principle of personnel management was inherited from the founder of Samsung, but reinforced in Lee's era, empowering managers to work more freely. Once a person is acknowledged to possess leadership and competence, he or she is given the responsibility to make decisions and can thus exercise his or her ability fully. According to the degree of achievement, a punishment or reward can then be applied.

4   Samsung Electronics' Strategy for the "Analog to Digital" Paradigm Shift

In the analog era, "competence" meant the accumulation of experience, technology, and diligence. The strength of Japanese companies was their large body of accumulated knowledge. However, the "analog to digital" shift caused the meaning of "competence" to change. The new digital "system-on-chip" approach meant that all circuits were already in a semiconductor chip, and the assembly of parts became easier, while failure rates decreased. In the digital era, "competence" involves developing a new product quickly, before anyone else does so. It has also become possible for smaller enterprises to create products of a similar quality to those of larger companies. With this in mind, Samsung Electronics has concentrated on maximizing the value added by brand image and marketing strategies (*Chosun Biz*, February 19, 2010).

Samsung Electronics' profitable products of the digital era include semiconductors, LCDs, LCD TVs, and mobile phones. It is no exaggeration to say that these goods are the result of carrying out a strategy based on taking advantage of the digital era. During the analog era, an architect would draw up an embodied idea for manufacturing. All the relevant information regarding material, size, shape, parts, and structure would be drawn in detail in a diagram. To convert this 2D information into 3D form, knowledge of graphics was essential. However, after the emergence of 3D CAD, graphics became unnecessary. Design information could be shown in 3D, and the people at work sites could operate as indicated. There is now no need to remake a test model repeatedly, as computer simulation can take care of the process instead (Hatamura and Yoshikawa, 2009, pp. 119–120).

In the digital era, similar products can be made anywhere by anyone because of technology generalization. Hence, simple ideas such as the "product out" approach, which presumes that customers always crave something better, are no longer valid, because in today's digital world, the market is diversified and customers' demands and restraints differ in different areas or seasons. As such, it is vital to focus on the concept of "market in."

"Market in" offers what customers desire (Hatamura and Yoshikawa, 2009, pp. 186–187).

How did Samsung Electronics manage to dominate the global market even though its technology was far behind that of Japanese companies? Mitarai (2005) explains the strategic approaches of Korean companies as follows:

> "Because Korean companies lack their own technology resources, first, they look for a promising new business field. Then they decide what technology need to be secured and to what extent the facility investment should be made, in order to reach the business scale they are aiming for in the market which has the opportunity for them to enter. Meanwhile, Japanese companies have the product-out thinking which builds a business with bottom-up taking advantage of their research-and-development resources."

This explains why the choices made by Korean companies have given them a competitive advantage in the digital era. There are four principles of digital business strategy that officers of Samsung Electronics believe in: foresight, preoccupation, initiative, and occupancy. Applying these principles involve: "foreseeing market shifts and moving forward to beat rival companies and occupying the market before anyone else" (*Korea Economic Daily*, 2002, p. 135).

5   Conclusion

A comparison of the global digital product market share of Samsung Electronics and that of other companies, by *The Nikkei*, is presented in Table 1.

Samsung Electronics entered the electrical industry later than its competitors. In order to minimize the technology gap as a result of the late entry, it introduced the advanced techniques used by American and Japanese companies. After implementing the technologies of other companies, it focused on its own technology development and tried to improve its ability in the relevant fields. While other companies were worrying about the Asian monetary crisis, IT recession, and European economic crisis, Samsung Electronics used these crises as opportunities. Samsung Electronics has now become the world's number one IT company, overtaking other leading companies such as Sony, Siemens, and HP. The driving force behind its success in the face of crisis can be attributed to several clear factors.

First, the company chose to discard non–value-added businesses, unnecessary expenses, and human resources during the IMF monetary crisis.

Table 1. Global market share (unit: %).

Items/year	2005			2011		
Smartphone	Nokia	Motorola	Samsung Elec.	Samsung Elec.	Apple	Nokia
	30.7	15.7	12.6	19.1	18.8	15.6
DRAM	Samsung Elec.	Hynix	Micron Tec.	Samsung Elec.	Hynix	Elpita
	28.5	16.2	15.9	42.2	23.0	13.1
Liquid Crystal TV	Sharp	Sony	Panasonic	Samsung Elec.	LG Elec.	Sony
	34.1	12.5	10.7	28.8	13.7	10.6
Liquid Crystal Panel	Samsung SDI	LG Philips	Sharp	LG Display	Samsung Display	Chimei
	18.7	15.4	12.3	22.4	21.2	15.2

Source: *The Nikkei* (July 19, 2005; July 29, 2012).

After that, a reorganization of the business and the institution was carried out as a management measure. Second, to pursue qualitative change in the business, Samsung focused on human innovation, process innovation, and product innovation. Third, Samsung overcame several crises by spreading profit, utilizing a diversified portfolio covering semiconductors, communication, home electric appliances, and computers. A balanced portfolio is increasingly becoming a strength in the digital era, in which digital products are assimilating with one another. Fourth, Samsung's self-controlling management, as a decision-making mechanism for controlling uncertainty, also played an important role in its approach to the crisis. In today's "speed era," where there is rapid change in everything, providing managers with responsibility and authority has greatly increased Samsung Electronics' competitiveness. Finally, the leadership of Kunhee Lee, who foresaw changes and correctly steered the large company down the right path, was invaluable.

This chapter examined the efforts made by Samsung Electronics during the "analog to digital" shift accompanying IT innovation in order to overcome the effects of the IMF monetary crisis. Companies are all regularly confronted with crises. Whether they succeed or not depends on how they face their difficulties.

Endnote

1. Compilation Committee of Samsung Electronics (2010). Available at: http://www.samsung.com/sec/aboutsamsung/; Accessed July 14, 2012; http://drat.fss.or.kr/dsab001/main.do?autoSearch=true. Accessed July 20, 2012.

References

Chosun Biz website (2010). Adviser Jongyong Yun said 'Samsung Electronics CEO 12 years'. Available at: http://news.chosun.com/site/data/html_dir/2010/19/2012021901202.html. Accessed February 19, 2010 (in Korean).

Compilation Committee of Samsung Electronics (2010). *Samsung Electronics — The History of 40 Years*, Seoul: Samsung Electronics (in Korean).

Etoday website. (2012). Samsung LG, OLED initiative of vertical integration, Available at: http://cn.moneta.co.kr/Service/stock/ShellView.asp?ModuleID=9539&LinkID=263&ArticleID=2012050911053401978&stockcode. Accessed May 9, 2012 (in Korean).

Hatamura, Y and R. Yoshikawa. (2009). *Management of a Crisis*, Tokyo: Kodanshya (in Japanese).

Korea Economic Daily (2002). *Samsung Rising*, Seoul: The Korea Economic Daily & Business Publication Inc (in Korean).

Korea Herald Business website (2012). Samsung Electronics, No. 1 market share in the first quarter, Available at: http://www.koreaheraldbiz.com/article.php?id=32228. Accessed April 2, 2012 (in Korean).

Lee, G. (2010). *The Story of Lee Kun-hee*, Seoul: Human & Books (in Korean).

Mitarai, H. (2005). The Change of the Management System of Korean Companies — The Strong Point of Decision-Making of Samsung Electronics, Tokyo: *Chisikisisansozo*, May 2005, 34–49 (in Japanese).

Money Today website (2011). Light and shadow of Vertical integration, Available at: http://news.mt.co.kr/mtview.php?no=2011060813398196563. Accessed June 14, 2011 (in Korean).

Son, H. (2011). *The Rewritten Economic Textbook*, Seoul: Joongang Books (in Korean).

The Nikkei (2005). Investigation of 24 Goods of a World Market Share, July 19 (in Japanese).

The Nikkei (2006). The Effect of Producing TV Components in-house, July 27 (in Japanese).

The Nikkei (2010). Remove the Spell of too Strong Quality, March 16 (in Japanese).

The Nikkei (2012). World Market Share, July 29 (in Japanese).

4

Activities of Cross-Functional Teams (CFTs) in Nissan: Considering from Revitalization Activities and their Results

Kazuki Hamada
Kwansei Gakuin University

1   Introduction

Today, an increasing number of companies need to be revitalized as they cannot adapt to recent abrupt changes in the business environment and the intensification of global competition. Revitalization aims to transform ailing companies into profitable enterprises. Some of these companies face bankruptcy, while others have major problems with financing and earning power. Some have liabilities that exceed their assets, a situation in which they have a negative net worth.

Companies that face major problems with their financing structure urgently require reforms if they are to survive and thrive without outside assistance. To this end, they must aim to reduce liabilities, gain earning power, and reinforce their net assets (equity capital) over the mid- and long-term, but they must also urgently consider whether a relief program involving a debt-for-equity swap, wherein a company hands its own stocks to creditors in exchange for reductions and exemptions for liability, is possible. Companies should examine the possibility of capital increases or capital injections with funds from banks, other companies, or employees. In some cases, it is necessary to examine the use of funds designed to promote corporate restructuring, the possibility of receiving public funds, and potential business alliances.

Once essential and urgent reforms have been made in the financing structures, business and management structure reforms aiming at increasing profits are necessary to ensure their survival. It is through this method that Nissan Motor Co. Ltd. was revived after going through a period of great financial difficulty in the 1990s. It first formed an alliance with Renault S.A.S., which helped with urgent financing restructuring, and then engaged in a process of continuous financial and business structure reform that it called the "Nissan Revival Plan (NRP)," which succeeded in regenerating the business. Nissan also reformed its management structure, enabling it to maintain high profits continuously after its revitalization had been accomplished. It did so by establishing a cross-functional team (CFT) management structure, which then became a significant feature of the company.

This chapter focuses on the CFTs that played an important role in the revival and subsequent growth of Nissan and considers their characteristics and the reasons for Nissan's success. Nissan's CFT management structures can be implemented to assist other companies; therefore, this chapter considers performance evaluation systems that can be employed in doing so.

2   Consolidated Financial Situation of Nissan and Capital Injection by Renault S.A.S.

2.1   *Financial situation before "Nissan Revival Plan" and capital injection by Renault S.A.S.*

After the Plaza Accord of 1985, the yen appreciated sharply, and Nissan settled its operating losses, with the resulting economic bubble improving the company's performance. Because of its positive capital spending, the aggregate amount of Nissan's current and fixed liabilities was 5,200 billion yen as of March 1992. Subsequently, the economic bubble burst, followed by severe serious recession. This aggravated Nissan's business problems, and although restructuring plans were made several times, its results did not bear fruit. In the 1992 fiscal year, the company's operating loss was 7 billion yen and its net losses were 56 billion yen. In the 1993 fiscal year, the company's operating loss was 144 billion yen and its net loss was 87 billion yen. In the 1994 fiscal year, the company's operating loss was 106 billion yen and its net loss was 166 billion yen. In the 1995 fiscal year, the company's operating income was 41 billion yen and its net loss 88 billion yen. Nissan's aggregate liabilities continued to increase gradually over this period, and it significantly increase its short-term and long-term borrowing.

By the 1996 fiscal year-end, Nissan's net income was 78 billion yen, based on increased demand in America and the depreciation of the yen. Although the performances of Toyota and Honda were good in the 1997 fiscal year, Nissan faced net losses of 14 billion yen, in spite of holding an operating income of 84 billion yen. Although the company announced a reorganization plan in 1998, and its operating income was 110 billion yen by the 1998 fiscal year-end, its net losses were 28 billion yen. Its aggregate liabilities gradually increased until March 1998, when both short-term and long-term borrowing had become very high.

The management of Nissan lacked focus in the 1990s, and the state of its financing deteriorated to such an extent that most banks decided not to relieve it anymore. As such, Nissan began to look for domestic and foreign partners, planning to restructure itself through a business partnership, and fortunately was able to form a partnership with Renault in March 1999. Renault invested 585.7 billion yen and purchased about 1,464 million new stocks of Nissan at the price of 400 yen per stock, giving it a shareholding ratio of 36.8%. Renault also purchased bonds with warrants that Nissan published for 216 billion yen, which enabled it to increase its shareholding ratio to 44.4% in the future. Renault also purchased 22.5% of the stock of Nissan Diesel Motor Co., a company affiliated with Nissan, for 9.3 billion yen, and acquired subsidiary stocks. It purchased a financial subsidiary for 38 billion yen (Nissan Motor, annual reports, 1985–2011).

Nissan received large-scale financial assistance through its alliance with Renault and was able to improve and reform its financial and business structure.

2.2 NRP and subsequent medium-term profit plans

In March 1999, the CEO of Renault nominated Carlos Ghosn as the CEO of Nissan, entrusting him with the job of rebuilding the company and implementing reforms to its business structure. Ghosn formulated the "Nissan Revival Plan (NRP)" (2000–2002 fiscal years), which was announced in October 1999. The goals of the plan were as follows (Yoshino and Egawa, 2010; Hatakeyama, 2006):

(1) In the 2000 fiscal year, swing into the black on a consolidated operating income.
(2) In the 2002 fiscal year, raise the consolidated operating income margin by more than 4.5%.

(3) By the fiscal year-end of 2002, reduce substantial interest-bearing debt in the car segment from 1,400 billion yen to 700 billion yen.

The concrete details of the plan are covered in more detail later in this chapter. The objectives were accomplished one year in advance of the target, in the 2001 fiscal year.

After the 2001 fiscal year, Nissan drew up the following medium-range profit plans, with the following objectives (Hatakeyama, 2006):

(1) "Nissan 180" (2002–2004 fiscal years)
   Goals:

   (1) By the fiscal year-end of 2004, increase global scales volume by 1 million.
   (2) By the fiscal year-end of 2004, achieve an 8% consolidated operating income margin.
   (3) By the fiscal year-end of 2004, achieve a substantial interest-bearing debt balance of zero in the car segment.

   Result: Nissan achieved all of its goals by 2004.

(2) "Nissan value up" (2005–2007 fiscal years)
   Goals:

   (1) In each of the three years of the plan, maintain a top-level operating income margin in the global car industry.
   (2) In the 2008 fiscal year, realize 4.2 million global sales volume.
   (3) During the period, maintain a return on invested capital (ROIC) of 20% (excluding cash on hand) on an average.

   Result: The achievement of the sales volume target delayed by one year; however, the operating income margin was high, and although the target ROIC (17%) could not be achieved, their ROIC was at the top level in the automotive industry.

(3) "Nissan GT 2012" (2008–2012 fiscal years)
   Nissan is committed to profit; however, it is not reflected in this medium-range plan, which involves profit targets only for the internal organization. The spirit of the commitment management is unchangeable.

G: Growth, T: Trust

   Goals:

   (1) Become a leader in quality by improving the quality of products, services, brand, and management.

(2) Become a leader in the zero-emission field, to start selling electric cars in the U.S. and Japan in the 2012 fiscal year, and to achieve large-scale sales worldwide in the 2012 fiscal year.

(3) Increase sales by 5% for five years, on an average, to start selling 60 new types of cars by 2012 fiscal year, and to add over 15 new technologies annually in the 2009 fiscal year.

(4) **"Nissan Power 88" (2011–2016 fiscal years)**
Goals:

(1) Improve brand power and sales power.
(2) Achieve 8% global market share by the 2016 fiscal year.
(3) Achieve a consolidated operating income margin of 8% by the 2016 fiscal year.

Nissan increased its aggregate liabilities slightly after implementing the NRP; however, it continued to make regular profits. However, after the September 2008 Lehman shock, Nissan fell into the red again and it was said that this was because it neglected its future investments by focusing too heavily on restructuring. However, its prior investments in China and focus on next-generation electric cars allowed it to achieve a rapid recovery.

3 Characteristics of CFTs and the Formulation of NRP in Nissan

The formulation and practice of the NRP offer clues as to the basis of the revival of Nissan. In this section, I consider the characteristics of CFTs that played an important role in this development. In order to reform business structures and revive Nissan, the company had to decide the way forward. Therefore, Ghosn inspected the company and conducted a hearing that enabled him to identify the gaps in Nissan. These were (1) intention of profit, (2) serious consideration of customers, (3) cross-intention of function and field, (4) sense of impending crisis, (5) common vision and long-term strategy.

In particular, Ghosn noticed that Nissan was very bureaucratic hierarchical, which he felt was the root of other problems. In order to overcome this, in July 1999, Nissan organized CFTs to resolve nine problems, which were (Hatakeyama, 2006, Yoshino and Egawa, 2010):

CFT#1 Business development   CFT#2 Purchasing
CFT#3 Production, distribution   CFT#4 Research and development

CFT#5 Marketing, sales   CFT#6 General management
CFT#7 Financial costs   CFT#8 Car model reduction
CFT#9 Organization and decision-making process

CFTs were necessary because they were important for the entire company to think about a solution if it hoped to achieve significant and timely results. As problems are often hidden between departments and organizations, it is necessary to have hierarchical management processes and solutions that consider the whole company. In addition, in a large company, the department where a problem occurs is sometimes different from the department where the problem is created.

The CFTs of Nissan were placed under the CEO and were made up of an average of approximately 10 members. They did not take responsibility for results, such as taskforces or project teams; however, they were organized to concentrate on providing suggestions. This was done because whenever CFTs were given the responsibility of the execution stage, constructive ideas did not emerge from the teams. The constitution of CFTs is shown in Fig. 1.

The duty of the leader is to act as an advising member, supporting other members and choosing a pilot. The pilot is a person who conducts the central activity of the CFT and is chosen from middle management, and holds his or her usual duties concurrently. The concrete activities of the CFT pilot are as follows.

(1) Problems setting
    The pilot clarifies the problems in the current organizational structure and business processes by comparing them with the company's

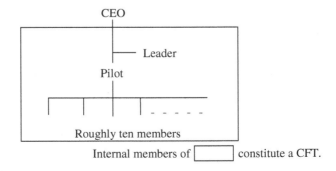

Fig. 1.   Constitution of each CFT in Nissan.

medium-range goals and decides on points that are inferior to rivals, and those that can improve sales and profit innovatively.

(2) Members choice

The pilot chooses departments and companies concerned with the investigation of causes and problems and finds people with the relevant expertise to troubleshoot. He or she sometimes asks for the recommendation of appropriate persons. A person from an associated company may be chosen as a member.

(3) Investigation of root causes

The pilot analyzes business processes and results based on data he or she holds and conducts brainstorming sessions with members. Based on the results, the pilot builds a hypothesis and investigates customers, other companies, and existing analyses before engaging in the process of brainstorming once again. The enforcement of benchmarking is effective in the investigation of root causes.

(4) Planning solutions and trial calculations of effect

Benchmarking and case studies of other companies help to determine solutions. The pilot calculates enforcement effects as numerical tests. When he or she cannot arrive at definite results, he or she engages in experimental practice through a pilot run. Suggestions made to the CEO are supported with numbers, and an executive committee chooses the solution that will be adopted.

There are also problems with CFTs. For example, their cross-functional variety introduces diverse perspectives and may produce creative solutions; however, this can make it difficult to arrive at a solution. Members often attach great importance to their positions, and introduce excessive information that can delay decisions. Conversely, unity among members is important to the functioning of CFTs; however, it may stifle originality.

Nissan utilized CFTs well, and these CFTs provided over 400 suggestions, forming the basis of a comprehensive plan drawn up by its executive committee, which was announced by Ghosn as the NRP in October 1999.

4   Concrete Contents of NRP

The plan was implemented after its announcement of NRP. It had two parts, one based on the reduction of interest-bearing debt to improve financial structure, and the other on cutting costs for profit security. Business structure reforms had to be conducted simultaneously.

4.1 *Sale of assets to reduce interest-bearing debt*

As mentioned above, the real interest-bearing debt of Nissan's business was 1,400 billion yen at the time of the NRP formulation. Cash was needed to pay back loans. The means of acquiring this cash were (1) the sale of assets and (2) profit acquisition. Nissan had to rely on asset sales for quick action because earning profits takes time. This involved the sale of securities, real estate, and assets other than its core car business. Nissan reduced its interest-bearing debt as much as possible by these means. In particular, it conducted the large-scale sale of short-team securities and affiliated company stocks. In those days, Nissan held more than 1,000 affiliated company stocks and had more than 20% shares in the majority of those companies. It was judged that stocks in only four companies were indispensable to the future of the company, and Nissan sold as many of its stocks as possible. Nissan also carried out the sale of affiliated companies (business transfer, assets scale, etc.), which was not a part of its core duties (Monden, 2005).

The sale of assets led to a reduction in Nissan's considerable interest-bearing debt; however, this only allowed for a temporary acquisition of cash, and the sequential acquisition of profit and reduction of interest-bearing debt then became necessary (Monden, 2009).

4.2 *Cutting costs to securing profits*

Increasing sales amounts or reducing costs allows a company to earn a profit. Nissan decided that it had to perform thorough performed cost cuts to gain immediate results. The resulting cost cuts led to an increase in sales through reduction in sales prices.

The improvement of workflows at the company was also a necessary part of cost cutting, which meant that the reform of functional departments was necessary, as actual operations were run by individual functional departments. The total cost structures of Nissan in 1998 were as follows (Monden, 2005):

Purchasing costs (direct material costs)	60%
Production costs (conversion costs)	11%
Research and development costs	3%
Distribution costs, general administrative expenses	23%
Other	3%

The ratio of purchasing costs to total costs was particularly high, making the reduction of costs crucial. The reduction of distribution costs and general administrative expenses were also important. Cost-cutting measures were enforced based on the suggestion of CFTs, including five characteristic items (Yoshino and Egawa, 2010).

(1) Reduction of direct materials (20% reduction in purchasing costs)

Nissan aimed to halve its number of suppliers to reduce purchasing costs. It hoped to realize economic efficiency of scale by increasing business with its remaining suppliers, making deals for increased quantities of orders that reduced purchase unit prices. It thus reviewed related companies and sorted suppliers based on their efficiency, not only within Japan but also from a global viewpoint. It also demanded effectiveness from its suppliers and rationalized procurement processes. Consequently, it surpassed its purchasing cost-cutting targets.

(2) Reduction of conversion costs

Conversion costs needed to be achieved in order to realize optimum production efficiency. As such, in order to improve its operations, Nissan closed factories that were not efficient, such as the Murayama factory of its head office, Kyoto factory of Nissan Shatai Co., Minato factory of Aich Kikai, and engine factories of Kurihama and Kyushu. Moreover, by intensifying and rationalizing the production organization, Nissan aimed to accomplish economic efficiency of scale.

(3) Reduction of distribution costs and general administrative expenses

Nissan aimed for a 20% reduction in distribution costs. It had a number of business bases that had low profitability because of serious share and number considerations. Therefore, it rationalized the distribution system and reduced the number of dealers under direct control, as well as the number of business offices that were not highly profitable, and cut rebates heavily. In particular, it conducted a rationalization of its North American area mechanism and the reorganization of its European dealer network.

(4) Use of research and development costs based on the priority principle

Nissan did not aim for the reduction of research and development costs, but for their effective utilization, as this area was important to the company's future development. It made the most of its core technologies while spending heavily on research and development. Nissan also reorganized to build a global development system. As a result, research and development costs decreased by 17%; however, the cost of the person engaged in new products and new technologies rose by 15%.

(5) Financial management

In order to reduce financial costs, Nissan introduced a cash management system. This system, which concentrates financial operations and is devised to manage finance and risks from the whole-group perspective, aims to manage funds in an efficient manner. It reduces procurement costs and financial risks by replacing borrowed money from subsidiaries with low-cost group funds.

5   CFT and V-up Activities

5.1   *Need for V-up activities*

By making the CFTs the driving force of NRP development, Nissan was able to revive itself. As mentioned earlier, there were initially nine CFTs, each of which had approximately ten members, meaning that the number of individuals directly involved in CFTs was relatively small. When quick changes were required, these small numbers were effective; however, for the next step after corporate revival, more employees were required. Therefore, thought processes of CFTs were applied to company-wide solutions to solve problems in the lower rungs of the organization. The "V-up" program, an operation improvement method that could be applied to every section, was devised and introduced in domestic and foreign Nissan groups in April 2001 (Nissan Motor, 2005).

The V-up program investigates problems in each section with over 400 employees in the main body of Nissan and involves solutions that take a maximum of six months. Using this strategy, the company had solved over 4,400 problems by March 2005.

The characteristics of the V-up program are as follows.

(1) Analytical tools are changed depending on the problem.
(2) Programs are divided into V-up and V-Fast based on their nature. V-up programs handle major problems that will take three to six months to resolve, whereas V-Fast deals with simpler problems that will take

roughly one month to solve. The head of each department decides which method will be used.

(3) Teams are organized across sections, because the problems in each section affect the other sections, and are in turn affected by them.

(4) A variety of root causes are suggested for each problem. These are suggested by CFTs, the management committees involved in domestic and foreign local business meetings, heads of departments, and subordinates, and through the "issue bank" suggestion boxes installed by the secretariat.

(5) Both goals and results are evaluated numerically. The accounting department employee, known as the "validator," is in charge of measurements and predicting the effects of solutions. The effects of V-up must be converted into financial values in all cases; however, this is not true for V-Fast. In addition, sets of two measures are always used, with the first measuring main purposes, and the second measuring the negative effects that may result from initial measures.

5.2 *V-up and V-Fast teams*

The members of a V-up team are as follows (Nissan, 2005):

V leader (one person, head or director or a department): Takes responsibility for the achievement of a solution.

V pilot (one person, section manager): Leads solution creation and is charged with expediting the proceedings of conferences. Not responsible for results, making it easier to propose original and bold ideas. Focuses on motivating team members and arriving at effective ideas.

V expert (one person): Supports V leader and V pilot, receives specialized training, and is next in line after V leader and V pilot.

V crew (six to eight people): Chosen from various sections.

Validator (one person): In charge of predicting effects and measuring enforcement results.

Although the V-up team proposes solutions for problems in individual sections, CFTs come up with solutions to company-wide problems, meaning that the roles of the two are different, although their members' roles are similar.

The V-up team's activities are as follows:

(1) The head or director of a department determines problems, which are submitted to a V leader by one of several routes. This person then

becomes a leader to examine the problems, appointing a subordinate as a V pilot.

(2) The V expert and validator work with the V leader and V pilot to determine problems and predict the financial effects of solving them.

(3) The V pilot chooses a V crew from across different sections to form a V-up team.

(4) The V-up team analyzes data in detail, identifies basic factors for solving problems, and develops effective policies for addressing the factors. Policies are examined and useful policies are decided.

(5) Line departments decide how to implement the policies that a V-up team has drafted.

(6) The validator measures the effects that implementing these policies will have and determines degrees of accomplishment. The validator continuously inspects effects over a period of approximately three years. The contents of activities are displayed on the company intranet.

The members of a V-Fast team are as follows:

Leader (one person): In charge of achieving a solution.

Facilitator (one person): In charge of suggesting solutions suggestion, preparing materials and agendas, acting as the chairman of a one-day intensive discussion, and putting together effective measures.

Expert (one person): Promotes solutions and advises.

Crew (six to eight people).

Validator (one person).

V-Fast team's activities are conducted in the following order:

(1) Problem setting.

(2) Team formation and preparation for intensive discussion.

(3) One-day intensive discussion session.

(4) Policy suggestion and execution by line departments.

(5) Fixation and evaluation.

5.3 *Interlocking activities of CFTs and V-up teams*

The CFT and V-up programs are the two wheels that support the Nissan management. The CFTs handle company-wide macro problems and report to the CEO. The V-up teams handle the smaller-scale problems in individual sections, and report on them to the head of their section. At the time of the development of the NRP, improvement efforts had only focused on

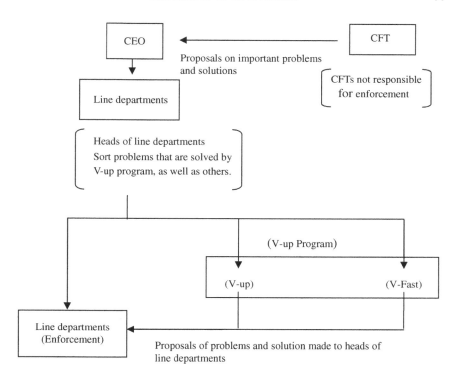

Fig. 2.   Relationships between CFTs and V-up programs.
(Adapted from Nissan Motor (2005) with modification.)

catching up with other companies. After the "Nissan 180" program got the company's revival on track, however, Nissan needed to address areas not covered by other companies. To that end, a system of organization that allowed for the fine analysis of problems was required (Hatakeyama, 2006). The V-up program helped to enable close correspondence.

Figure 2 depicts the relationships between the CFTs and V-up programs. The CEO of the company receives suggestions related to company-wide problems and their solutions from CFTs, decides on an enforcement plan, and gives permission to the line departments to initiate practice. Problems can then arise in the implementation of the plan in the line departments. In this case, the departments examine the problems and solutions through the V-up program, using either V-up or V-Fast. After solutions are suggested to the heads of the line departments and decided upon, the line departments will implement them.

6 Performance Evaluation System for Effective CFT Activities

6.1 *Importance of process evaluation indexes*

Nissan's CFTs do not take responsibility for enforcement; however, it is thought that it is necessary to design the performance evaluation system which reports the state of the practice of line departments and the result to CFTs. Therefore, I will consider a desirable performance evaluation system that is useful for CFTs. The performance evaluation system that I will mention in this section is not the example of Nissan. Traditional systems of performance evaluation are not suitable to these process evaluations, as they only measure the result of individual departments, enabling managers to understand the degree to which goals have been achieved, but not how they have been accomplished.

As CFTs are in charge of solutions to cross-sectional problems, they must capture the connection between departments, which implies that both result measures and process evaluation measures are important to them. Process evaluation measures evaluate the situation of the means to bring about results (leading indicators), whereas result measures evaluate the results of business activities (lagging indicators). Evaluating problems only through result measures makes timely responses difficult which is why process evaluation measures are required (Horonec, 1993; Meyer, 2005).

The specific advantages of using process evaluation measures are as follows:

(1) Managers can understand achievement situations in a precise and timely manner.
(2) If a problem occurs, causes can be immediately examined.
(3) Managers can foresee and prevent problem.
(4) Process improvement is continuously motivated.

6.2 *The relationship between process evaluation measures and result measures*

A good evaluation of the leading indicator of a process is not necessarily tied to a good result measure (result target), which is why managers need to understand the relationships between process evaluation measures and result measures, and to manage these relationships for the achievement of result targets.

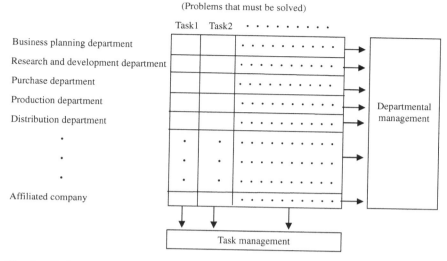

Fig. 3. Relationships between task management and departmental management.

Result targets involve both task goals and department goals, which makes it necessary to clarify the relationship between process evaluation measures and task goals, and between process evaluation measures and department goals. Task goals are accomplished based on the efficiency of each related department; however, employees come to ignore this when they are overly focused on the achievement of individual tasks, which is why task management and departmental management are necessary. CFT requires the achievement of both department and task goals to be considered, implying that appropriate matrix performance evaluation systems are important.

Figure 3 depicts the thought process involved in the matrix performance evaluation system. Task management involves considering the mutual relationships between departments and it is shown vertically. Departmental management considers the mutual relationships between tasks within departments, and it is shown horizontally. Management involving both of these directions employs process evaluation measures as well as result measures.

Effective management uses a balanced scorecard (BSC) that considers the relationships between process evaluation measures and result measures. Management by BSC accomplishes the processes and results by considering the relationships between measures and deploys strategic goals to address important financial and non-financial measures. To make causation clear, a strategic map that effectively shows the routes to achieving strategies and causation among strategic measures should be used.

BSCs should be applied to a matrix performance evaluation system to manage CFTs. To use BSCs, it is necessary to choose the appropriate measures and to clarify the following:

(1) Relationships between process evaluation measures and result measures in departmental management.
(2) Relationships in task management.
(3) Mutual relationships between departmental process evaluation measures and task management.
(4) Mutual relationships between result measures in departmental management and task management.

7 Summary

Various factors have enabled the corporate revival of Nissan and its ongoing growth; however, several of these are of particular importance (Ueda, 2011). The first is Ghosn's brilliance as a CEO and his objective work on management reform through a zero-base review. Ghosn made his visions plain, evident, and clear, and he effectively communicated them to the whole Nissan group. In the investigation of the causes of Nissan's management crisis, he considered on-site opinions and made much of the analyses based on facts. In the discovery of problems and the search for solutions, he used CFTs effectively (Urushihara, 2012).

The second factor in Nissan's success was its bold cost-cutting measures and decisions and its reduction plan for employees. To that end, mergers and acquisitions were enforced, and the large-scale organization was reorganized. It is worthy of attention that Ghosn invested in techniques and products with a bright future while simultaneously pushing reforms forward; however, it is also clear that he would not have been able to allot funds to technology development without prioritizing the improvement of the company's financial standing.

The third factor was the appropriate communication of a profit-oriented perspective to employees through the CFT system, which improved the overall communication in the company and employee consciousness.

The fourth factor was the adoption of performance evaluation systems that were consistent with maximization of profits, and the carrying out of appropriate evaluations of results.

In this chapter, I focus on the effective use of CFTs, which is the most important factor in Nissan's success, and not the detailed consideration of all the aforementioned factors. I also compare effective usage of CFTs and their original usage by Nissan. After going through a corporate revival, Nissan implemented the V-up program to solve problems in individual sections, effectively connecting the program to the CFT system.

The cross-functional management described in this chapter is not only carried out by Nissan, but many other companies, including Toyota, which recognized the importance of the formulation and enforcement of broad overall corporate strategies and goals, as well as the combined wisdom of companies, departments, and employees. It is important that such strategies are individualized to suit particular companies, but I feel that Nissan's example can serve as a crucial point of references in this process.

References

Hatakeyama, D. (2006). Cross-functional teams in Nissan: Summary of activities and recent trends, in Kenkyukai, K. (ed.), *From "Choice/concentration" to "Realization of the Next Growth Strategy": A Case Book of Management, Innovation, Promotion and Practices*, Tokyo: Kigyo Kenkyukai, pp. 163–174 (in Japanese).

Horonec, S. M. (1993). *Vital Signs: Using Quality, Time, and Performance Measurements to Chart your Company's Future*, New York: American Management Association.

Meyer, C. (2005). How the right measures help teams excel, in Diamond Harvard Business Review editorial department, (ed.), *Creating a High-Performance Organization*, Tokyo: Diamond, pp. 119–145 (in Japanese).

Monden, Y. (2005). *Organization Design and Management Accounting for Corporate Value Improvement*, Tokyo: Zeimu Keiri Kyokai (in Japanese).

Monden, Y. (2009). *Management Change to Overcome Recession*, Tokyo: Zeimu Keiri Kyokai (in Japanese).

Nissan Motor, (2005). The power of V-up program as a cross-functional operation improvement method: Groups and tens of thousands of employees become "Ghosn", *Nikkei Jyoho Strategy*, 56–73 (in Japanese).

Nissan Motor, (1985–2011FY). *Annual Reports*, Nissan Motor (ed.), Nissan Motor (in Japanese).

Ueda, O. (2011). *Seven Inviolable Rules of Corporate Revitalization*, Tokyo: Nihon Keizai Shinbunsha (in Japanese).

Urushihara, J. (2012). *Marvel Meetings in Nissan: Know-how Produced by Ten Years of Reform,* Tokyo: Toyo Keizai Shinposha (in Japanese).

Yoshino, Y. and Egawa, M. (2010). Nissan Motor: The challenge of revitalizing, in Harvard Business School (ed.), *Case studies, Japanese Companies Case Book*, Tokyo, Japan Business Research Center, pp. 33–67 (in Japanese).

5

Overcoming the Business Crisis by Applying Capital Cost Management: Case Study of the Panasonic Group

Shufuku Hiraoka
Soka University

1 Introduction

The purpose of corporate group management is to ensure sustainability. Panasonic Group, which is a part of the electronic industry in Japan, is restructuring its business domains in the face of the greatest business crisis since World War II. Panasonic is in keen competition with other Asian companies in the global market. For example, in the liquid crystal television business, Panasonic is facing severe competition from South Korean companies. Moreover, the appreciation of yen currency has considerably reduced Panasonic's sales and income. The liquid crystal panel factory in Chiba prefecture was damaged by the 2011 Tohoku earthquake and tsunami. Hence, the Panasonic Group is adopting management accounting systems that will enable it to restructure its business domains to face the challenges of this business crisis.

Panasonic has been using the management accounting system termed "Capital Cost Management" (CCM) since 1999 (Hiraoka, 2006). However, Panasonic's net loss for the 2011 fiscal year exceeded 772 billion yen. One reason for this loss was that Panasonic failed to sufficiently exploit the usefulness of CCM. For example, a series of large plant investments for manufacturing televisions and other devices fell through. Therefore, I will review how CCM can be used most effectively by relating it to the changes in the Panasonic Group. The consolidated financial statements of Panasonic Group revealed that its financial risk increased after the ownership of all the stocks of Panasonic Electric Works (Hiraoka, 2010a) and SANYO

Electric passed to Panasonic Electric Industrial. It is essential that Panasonic Group establish a more sound capital structure in the future; CCM would also be useful for this purpose. In this chapter, I will clarify how challenges that the business crisis poses for Panasonic could be overcoming by using CCM in their restructuring activities.

2 Panasonic's Restructuring Activities and Strategies in Recent Years

Panasonic needs to restore stability to its financial performance measures immediately and should pursue the following objectives for accomplishing this task:

- Attaching importance to profitability,
- Thoroughgoing cash flow management, and
- Reshaping of the financial base.

All the above-mentioned objectives are closely related to CCM, and this system should be used in any efforts to restore the company's financial performance.

The large end-of-year loss for the fiscal year 2011 was mainly due to the following restructuring expenses:

- Retirement and business restructuring expenses: Approximately 148 billion yen.
- Close out and impairment losses related to fixed assets: Approximately 334 billion yen.
- Impairment loss and others related to goodwill: Approximately 285 billion yen.

Business items on the accounts comprise approximately 290 billion yen for the AVC Networks segment, approximately 94 billion yen for the device segment, and approximately 384 billion yen for other segments. The AVC Networks segment mainly deals with televisions. The restructuring expenses account for sunk costs arising from decision-making errors in the past. It was essential for Panasonic to disclose these restructuring expenses early on, because Panasonic wanted to eliminate sunk costs in the future. It would be reasonable to say that the real restructuring of Panasonic began only after this disclosure. The restructuring of Panasonic involved reexamining and reshaping its existing businesses, developing new business models, and redesigning the organization to reduce costs and increase sales.

Panasonic adopted a new domain system after integrating the Electric Industrial, Electric Works, and SANYO Electric divisions. The new domain system consists of the following three business areas: "Global Consumer (B to C)," "Global Solution (B to B)," and "Global Device (B to B)." Each of these business areas has some business domains. Global Consumer comprises AVC Networks (AVC) and Appliance (AP). Global Solution comprises System Communications (SNC), Eco Solutions (ES), Health Care (HCC), and Manufacturing Solutions (MS). Global Device comprises Automotive Systems (PAS), Device (ID), and Energy (EC). Each business domain corresponds to each business segment, based on the "Management Approach" described in the financial reports released to the public (Hiraoka, 2010b), with the exception of HCC and MS, which are included in the items recorded under others. In the fiscal year 2011, Panasonic's profit and loss statement showed a deficit; however, we can observe mutual aid among the domains when we analyze segment cash flow information, as shown in Table 1:

Since Panasonic uses the U.S. accounting standards, it does not disclose the working capital information of each segment/domain. Therefore, since this information was not available, we used the following equation to obtain the approximate cash flow of each segment/domain:

The cash flow of segment = operating profit

$$\times \, (1 - \text{the prescribed effective tax rate})$$

$$+ \, \text{depreciation cost} - \text{capital expenditure.}$$

In the fiscal year 2011, the net cash outflows of AVC and ID were compensated by the net cash inflows of the other domains. However, the cash in hand and cash in bank substantially decreased because Panasonic needed to pay off bonds and head office expenses company wide in the fiscal

Table 1.   The cash flow of Panasonic's business domains: Yen (millions).

Business domains	2011.4~2012.3	2010.4~2011.3
AVC Networks (AVC)	−35,473	−53,728
Appliance (AP)	36,742	50,074
System Communications (SNC)	9,484	23,944
Eco Solutions (ES)	37,367	36,676
Automotive Systems (PAS)	4,264	16,107
Device (ID)	−9,629	38,556
Energy (EC)	561	−14,244
Others	20,182	38,715

year 2011. Therefore, Panasonic's performance in the recent years has not been good, and the company needs to improve its financial performance immediately. To this end, Panasonic has been restructuring and engaging in various strategies, which are detailed in the following paragraph.

The AVC domain reduced its fixed costs by consolidating some of the plasma television panel manufacturing plants. AVC began focusing on select television sets that have a higher profitability and eliminated those with lower profitability. AVC will develop new markets for liquid crystal televisions. Panasonic also decided to cooperate with SONY in the Organic Electro-Luminescence (OEL) TV business, and further pursue the avionics business (AV in aircrafts).

The ID domain reduced its fixed costs by downsizing the surplus of fixed assets. The company's film capacitors and high-density interconnections for smart phones (ALIVH) have already proved competitive on the world market. To extend its market share, ID has been expanding its scale of production in China and Vietnam. Panasonic has decided to develop the LSI system through joint partnership. The partners are FUJITHU and Renesas Electronics. The investor is The Innovation Network Corporation of Japan. Panasonic takes charge of the design. They purchased the plant of Elpida Memory in Hiroshima prefecture for producing. The strategy is a kind of asset light. The company will also develop a next-generation semiconductor memory.

Panasonic has been creating some new business models in the ecological and energy businesses. It is necessary for Panasonic to reinforce and grow its ES business, because ES will increase the market share of LED by meeting the demand for replacements. Panasonic can lower the cost and the price of business-use LED with suppressing power consumption and light for saving energy. Panasonic established a new division responsible for LED safety, which cooperates with the sales staff to increase the sales of LED. Panasonic also established a promotional team for developing the ecological management system and a new unit named "The head office of Marugoto Solutions" for ES. "*Marugoto*" means the whole house, whole office, whole store, whole building, and whole town. This is a strategy to provide many products related to the environment — home electronics for saving energy, solar batteries, condensers, storage batteries, and security devices — as part of a unified effort by the Panasonic Group to solve its business and financial problems. Panasonic is in the process of creating 100 new business models related to Marugoto Solutions termed "100 arrows." Each business model is estimated to yield sales of approximately 10 billion yen, and Panasonic aims to avoid business risk through these strategies.

Among as the domains, AP's return on sales is the highest for the Panasonic Group. AP has been reinforcing its competitiveness in North America and Asia and has promoted the localization of production and development in India, Brazil, Nigeria, and Vietnam. Panasonic considers hair dryers and shavers as effective products for entering appliance markets because South Korean companies are weak in these areas.

EC is responsible for the storage battery business and the solar system business. The main products of the storage battery business are lithium-ion and nickel metal hydride, and these batteries give Panasonic a competitive edge over South Korean companies in terms of supplying batteries for clean cars, electric cars, and hybrid cars. In China, Panasonic established a lithium-ion battery plant for smartphones and tablet-type devices. Panasonic also decided to produce lithium-ion batteries for the Volkswagen factory in Slovakia. Solar system plants were established in China and Malaysia to reduce costs. Panasonic has been making efforts to improve one of their products called "HIT," which increases the efficiency of energy conversion. It is Panasonic's endeavor to capture a market share of 35% in Japan. EC has been developing a system for combining the above-mentioned storage batteries with the solar system. The company has also reorganized the sales offices and reduced costs and has begun using feed-in tariff and subsidy programs in Japan.

SNC has transferred the entire cell phone business to China and Malaysia. Panasonic has re-entered the European market with the OEL screen and plans to develop the Asian and American markets. Panasonic has also acquired a security system company in India to expand the sales network for its security systems.

Further, Panasonic has entered the business of interior finishing and decorating for high-net-worth individuals in China. It has been employing the automatic welding system to save energy in China and India because of a shortage of electrical power in those countries. Panasonic has been increasing the local content ratio of materials and components from 60% to 80% in China and India in an effort to reduce costs.

Over the years, the executive compensation in Panasonic has been showing a downward trend; the compensations of the chairman and the president have been slashed by 70% and those of the directors and vice-president have been slashed by approximately 80%. Panasonic has been standardizing its salary and personnel system. Moreover, the company has introduced a common Web service using cloud computing, thereby enabling their 200,000 employees worldwide to simultaneously access and exchange information.

However, Panasonic has also been reducing their personnel. Recently, they reduced their workforce from 385,000 to 330,767 over a period of one and a half years. Many support subdivisions are being separated from the head office, such as information systems, office administration, manufacturing technology, and research and development. These subdivisions will be restructured and combined into a professional business support subdivision. The company plans to reduce the number of employees in the head office by half. The first 1000 people among those being made redundant will consist of the employees wishing to retire. The head office will be renamed the "corporate strategy head office" and the number of staff will be reduced to 150. Only three departments, Management Planning, Accounting & Finance, and a portion of the Personnel department, will continue to exist at the head office. Therefore, CCM will be strengthened in the new management control system. The activities related to CCM are summarized as follows:

- Revamping and reinforcing the existing businesses,
- Reducing costs related to the investment,
- Adjusting each business in each country to reduce costs and increase sales,
- Redefining business domains,
- Developing new business prospects, and
- Redesigning organizations.

Some signs of recovery of Panasonic's business are evident when we observe Panasonic's financial statement and segment information of the first quarter in the fiscal year 2012. The percentage of return on sales (ROS) for all business domains, except for SNC, was positive. However, these are short-range improvements. As for many strategies described above, we will also need to observe the financial achievements in the future. Panasonic's next goal is to entrench CCM as a positive value, because it improves capital efficiency and shareholder value.

3   Change in the Use of CCM from a Performance Management System to a Total Management System

CCM is a system for emphasizing the cost of capital in a company; Panasonic refers to this system as EVA® (Stewart, 1991; Young and O'Byrne, 2001; Hiraoka, 2007). CCM represents a type of residual income and it has traditionally been used as a management accounting system. When CCM was introduced in the Panasonic Group, it was calculated follows (Hiraoka, 2006):

CCM = operating profit + dividend received − cost of invested assets.

The cost of invested assets was calculated as follows:

Cost of invested assets = cost rate of invested assets × invested assets.

The invested assets were calculated by the following equation:

Invested assets = total assets − financial assets.

The cost rate of invested assets was calculated in the following manner:

Cost rate of invested assets = (interest + dividend + capital gain) ÷ invested assets.

When CCM was first introduced at Panasonic, the performance measure weight to evaluate the business units/divisions was 10%. After the divisions above 100 were concentrated in 17 business domains in 2002, the weight was raised by 50%. Panasonic has been raising the performance measure weights related to CCM by 60% since 2011. Currently, the managers of the business domains are also evaluated based on the performance measure weight. The items comprising the performance measure weight are as follows:

- The achievement rate of goal operating profit (5%).
- The improvement rate to net profit before tax of previous year (15%).
- The goal inventory to compress (10%).
- The achievement rate of free cash flow (5%).
- The improvement rate of free cash flow of previous year (15%).

About 30% of the weight is evaluated by sales and 10% is evaluated by the reduction of CO_2 emissions, besides CCM. The equation for calculating CCM has been redefined and is currently calculated using the following equation:

CCM = business profit − cost of invested assets.

Business profit = net profit before tax − interest earned + interest paid.

The cost of invested assets is as follows:

Cost of invested assets = cost rate of invested assets × invested assets.

The invested assets are derived from the business domain's consolidated balance sheet, as follows:

Invested assets = account receivable + inventory + foreign investment debt
= debt + shareholder's equity − cash on hand and at banks.

The cost rate of invested assets is as follows:

$$\text{Cost rate of invested assets} = (\text{interest} + \text{dividend} + \text{capital gain})$$
$$\div \text{invested assets.}$$

Since Panasonic uses the U.S. accounting standards, recurring profit does not appear on Panasonic's income statement. Despite restructured items being processed as extraordinary profit and loss items by Japanese Accounting Standards, in Panasonic, these restructuring items are included in the normalized profit before tax of each business domain. Panasonic reforms its business structure daily. However, when the restructuring policies of the head office incur high costs, Panasonic often excludes them from the profit before tax of each business domain.

The meaning of CCM is consistent with the aims of residual income (Solomons, 1965), which are as follows:

- Precisely recognizing the costs of the funds from stockholders and creditors.
- Improving both the income statement and balance sheet because of the maximization of CCM.
- Promoting the maximization of the cash flow.

The weights assigned to each of the performance evaluating items of CCM are high; this is done to set a benchmark and incentivize the business domain managers of the existing businesses and the new businesses to achieve the above-mentioned aims.

CCM is used to decide on business withdrawals. However, "the internal capital system" is applied to new businesses. Panasonic has been effectively using this system since 1954 and uses it along with the internal interest system. The internal capital is calculated as follows:

$$\text{Standard working capital} = \text{current assets} - \text{current liabilities}$$
$$\text{Internal capital} = \text{standard working capital}$$
$$+ \text{fixed assets} - \text{provision}$$
$$\text{Division net profit} = \text{division operating profit}$$
$$+ \text{internal interest earned}$$
$$- \text{internal interest paid} - \text{internal dividend}$$
$$- \text{corresponding tax.}$$

Either the entire net profit of a division or a part thereof is incorporated into the surpluses of the division. Panasonic once set the surpluses of divisions to zero when the new domain system was started. The use of CCM and the internal capital system enables the company to approach decision making in a manner that is suitable to the characteristics of the business. When using them, the heads of the domains and the division managers can ascertain the proper standard for the fixed assets and inventories.

4 The Linkage of CCM and the Drivers of Various Fields

CCM enables a company to improve cash flow and return on assets. It has enabled Panasonic to not only economize the balance sheet but also increase its corporate value. The company's executives are always looking for ways to increase their total profit and reduce the cost of invested assets to improve CCM. Business managers seek to identify ways to improve the rate of marginal profits, return on foreign investment, revenue of intangibles, and finances for increasing the total profit. They also look for ways to reduce the fixed costs and expense of intangibles, and improve finances. On the other hand, business managers strive to improve the turnovers of account receivables, inventory, and fixed assets for reducing the cost of invested assets.

The department managers find ways to increase the selling prices and the volumes. They consider and examine how they can reduce the costs of materials, costs of expanding sales, and physical distribution costs to improve the rate of marginal profit. They explore ways to reduce their labor costs, outlay costs, sales credits, and inventories and investigate ways to improve the product mix.

The personnel in various fields develop and sell the epoch-making new products that enable the company to raise its prices. They promote the internal development, worldwide purchasing, central buying, value engineering, and total quality management, and re-evaluate suppliers with a view to reducing material costs. To reduce the costs of expanding sales, these personnel reduce the amount of unsold stocks and sort the products. They accomplish this by taking the following measures:

- Concentrating the offices to reduce the physical distribution costs.
- Promoting ICT to reduce the physical distribution costs.
- Improving purchasing to reduce the physical distribution costs.
- Reducing the inventories to reduce the physical distribution costs.
- Shifting emphasis to the cash cows and the product stars for improving the product mix.
- Reducing the quality loss costs to improve the rate of marginal profit.
- Utilizing and cutting excess employees to reduce personnel expenses.
- Improving productivity to reduce personnel expenses.
- Outsourcing to reduce personnel expenses.

- Reorganizing and concentrating the offices to reduce personnel expenses.
- Restraining capital expenditures to reduce the expenses related to fixed assets.
- Buying and disposing of dormant assets to reduce the expenses related to fixed assets.
- Hastening collection to reduce sales credit.
- Reducing the lead time for reducing inventories.
- Reducing the unsold stocks to reduce the inventories.
- Improving the overall equipment efficiency and the operating ratio to raise the fixed assets turnover.
- Promoting shift work to raise the fixed assets turnover.

The contents cited above provide an outline of the system of management by objectives, which can also serve as a strategy map based on CCM. For example, a part of this map can be expressed as in Fig. 1 (the others are omitted). People in various fields can recognize the targets given as tools for working with the CCM system (Kawakami, 2012).

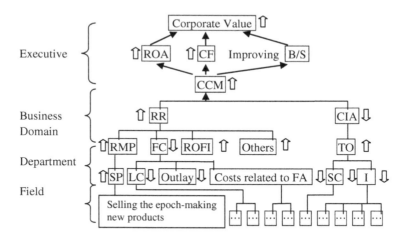

ROA: return on assets   CF: cash flow   B/S: balance sheet
RR: rate of return   CIA: cost of invested assets
RMP: rate of marginal profit   SP: selling price   FC: fixed costs
ROFI: return on foreign investment   TO: turnover
LC: labor costs   FA: fixed assets   SC: sales credits
I: inventories and capital investment

Fig. 1.   An example of management by objectives in CCM.

5 Conclusion

Broadly, CCM is the system for profit and cash management at Panasonic. The cost of capital contains not only the interest paid but also the return expected by the stockholders. In the light of the balance sheet debit, Panasonic has been calling it "the cost rate of invested assets," which it sets at 8.4%. The effect of CCM has been extended to the decision-making on business restructuring. In principle, if the CCM of the business results remains in a continuous deficit for over three years, the business must exit the market. CCM is a more concise and easier system than EVA®. Panasonic has connected CCM to the incentive system. When using the following equation, each business value can be expressed by the CCM of each business theoretically.

$$BV = IA + \sum_{i=1}^{n} \frac{CCM_i}{(1+c)^i},$$

where

BV: business value
CCM_i: CCM of period i
IA: initial invested assets of period 1
c: cost rate of invested assets
n: service life of business.

Creating the CCM of a business in the future will result in the creation of business value. Corporate value depends on all business values. To create corporate value, the strategies that worked best in each business life cycle must be executed. Panasonic will need to see the result of the long-range application of CCM for over three years. In addition to, we propose that Panasonic will use CCM with Business Portfolio Management and the business lifecycle because Panasonic will need to judge the continuation or abolition of each business with long-range viewpoint. We expect that Panasonic will overcome the current business crisis by maximizing the potential of CCM, thereby benefiting from the experience of failure in the past.

References

Hiraoka, S. (2006). Valuation of business based on EVA-Type metrics in Japanese companies, in *Value-Based Management of the Rising Sun,* eds. Monden, Y., Miyamoto, K., Hamada, K., Lee, G. and Asada. T., pp. 75–87, Singapore: World Scientific.

Hiraoka, S. (2007). Changes in the concept of capital and their effects on economic profit in Japan, in *Japanese Management Accounting Today*, eds. Monden, Y., Kosuga, M., Nagasaka, Y., Hiraoka, S. and Hoshi, N., Singapore: World Scientific, pp. 23–34.

Hiraoka, S. (2010a). Business valuation of a company group in Japan: A case study of segment reporting by Panasonic Electric Works, in *Business Group Management in Japan*, Hamada, K. (eds.), Singapore, World Scientific, pp. 105–118.

Hiraoka, S. (2010b). *The Study of Financial Metrics for Corporate and Business Valuation*, Tokyo: So-sei-sya (in Japanese).

Kawakami, T. (2012). *Frame of Mind for CFO, as a Right-hand Person to CEO: The Textbook of Cash Management by The Konosuke Matsushita Style*, Tokyo: Nihon keizai Sinbunsya (in Japanese).

Stewart, G. B. III. (1991). *The Quest for Value: The EVA^{TM} Management Guide*, New York: Harper Business.

Solomons, D. (1965).*Divisional Performance: Measurement and Control*, New York: Financial Executive Research Foundation.

Young, S. D. and O'Byrne, S. F. (2001). *EVA$^®$ and Value-Based Management: A Practical Guide to Implementation*, New York: McGraw-Hill.

PART 3

Coping with Business Crisis Applying the New Managerial Accounting

6

Basic Theory of Management for the Business Crisis

Akira Miyama
Kwansei Gakuin University

1 Introduction

Companies in Germany in the late 1970s suffered a serious business crisis due to the slow market and faced an urgent need to introduce effective business crisis management measures. A rapid increase in the number of bankrupt companies required the public sector to introduce drastic revisions of the bankruptcy law and procedures.

The increasing demand for crisis management strategies in the business world resulted in an increase in research and studies on business crisis management in the 1990s. Most of these studies were conducted by businessmen and consultants. In reality, few of the studies had a firm logical foundation; they merely advocated business crisis management efforts. It was not until recently that sophisticated theories on business crisis management appeared, with some even being innovative, presenting completely new theories. However, in my opinion, discussions on business crisis management are still at the development stage even today. Also, business crisis management has not yet been successfully explained in a systematic manner. I believe it is important to establish a systematic analysis of business crisis management that is based on a firm logical foundation.

2 Crises and Business Crises

2.1 *Concept of crisis*

The word "crisis" ("*Krise*" in German) can be used in various ways. When we use the terms "personal crisis" or "global crisis," the word "crisis" can be interpreted in many different ways. The concept of a "crisis," originating from the Greek word "*krisis*," was introduced by the German people in the 16th century, originally as a medical term to imply a "critical phase" (*Höhepunkt*) or a "transition stage" (*Wendepunkt*) in the progress of an illness (Apitz, 1987, S. 13). Accordingly, it referred to the time when important decisions relevant to the recovery or death of a patient had to be made. In the world of jurisprudence, the term "crisis" was often used in the context of "justice" (*Recht*) or "injustice" (*Unrecht*)" and in theology, it referred to "relief" (*Heil*) or "hellish punishment" (*Verdamnis*). Later in the 18th century, the concept was influenced by the French term "*crise*," which means a critical, difficult situation or predicament, and accordingly, the term "crisis" came to be defined as a situation involving an important decision or a turning point. Thus a crisis can be construed as a turning point, where both the opportunity for a breakthrough (*Chance*) and danger (*Gefahr*) coexist (Saynisch, 1994, S. 52). We can say that a crisis requires a decision to be made and that the situation can be characterized by the presence of dual potentials and ambivalence (Linde, 1987, S. 3; Krystek, 1987, S. 3). This viewpoint plays an important role in the analysis of business crises.

2.2 Concept of a business crisis

Recent research on business crises tends to focus on ultimate or important corporate goals, where strategic factors and the potential for attaining corporate targets are often talked about. With this in mind, this section discusses the concept of a "business crisis."

Usually, a business crisis becomes detectable when any "abnormal circumstance or a failure to attain a specific target" is revealed (Bergauer, 2003, S. 4). So failure to achieve an ultimate or important corporate goal is a typical situation in a business crisis. Here, "ultimate or important goals" cover profit targets and satisfy the liquidity requirements that are relevant to the survival of the business. Any event which impedes the achievement of these goals is considered to be a potential factor in causing a "business crisis." We can say that such an impediment is the primary attribute and could be the direct cause of a business crisis.

In addition, there are four secondary attributes of business crises (Schreyögg, 2004, S. 14; Müller, 1982, S. 6; Krystek, 1987, S. 6). They are: (1) unexpectedness, (2) endangered survival, (3) urgency for introducing countermeasures, and (4) diversity of causes. In other words, a business crisis can be defined as an unexpected situation that impedes the achievement of ultimate or important corporate goals and could eventually endanger the business itself. Such a situation does not give the business time to introduce countermeasures, and usually there exist multiple causes and complications behind such a situation.

Thus the occurrence of a business crisis is never sudden. It has been said that "a business crisis does not come overnight, but is preceded by a year-long, slow development of events," (Brühl, 2004, S. 5) and also that "a business crisis is often the result of a long-term accumulation of environmental changes concurrent with mismanagement by corporate managers" (KfW Bankgruppe, 2005, S. 11). In this light, to understand a business crisis, it is necessary to focus on the history of its development, segment it into phases, and clarify what happened in each phase.

Generally, a business crisis can be segmented into four phases which are respectively characterized by the existence of: (1) a potential threat (*potenzielle Unternehmungskrise*), (2) a latent threat (*latente Unternehmungskrise*), (3) a visible but controllable threat (*akute/beherrschbare Unternehmungskrise*), and (4) an apparent and uncontrollable threat (*akute/nicht beherrschbare Unternehmungskrise*) (Miyama 2010, p. 180 ff.; Krystek 2006, S. 48 ff.).

A "potential threat" (in Phase 1) can be defined as a danger which could develop into a critical problem in the future. In this phase, there are no detectable symptoms of the crisis in general, and the business organization looks sound and healthy, although technically we call this state "quasi-normal." In this phase, it is important for the organization to be aware of the potential threat without delay and implement the necessary measures in a strategic manner.

A "latent threat" (in Phase 2) can be defined as hidden danger which would most probably surface in the near future. Compared to Phase 1, early detection of the crisis symptoms in Phase 2 is not so important. However, early and appropriate recognition of the symptoms in this phase would help find effective countermeasures.

In Phase 3, with a "visible but controllable threat," the existence of a threat has been revealed and critical impacts are directly foreseeable. In this phase, early detection of the crisis symptoms does not help, but it is possible to overcome the difficult situation through a comprehensive input of resources to correct the situation and build up organizational resistance to problems. There is a turning point in Phase 3, at which successful implementation of countermeasures could save the organization and result in rehabilitation, whilst failure would result in bankruptcy. It should be also noted that there exists a second turning point which applies to bankrupt companies seeking reconstruction possibilities.

If an organization fails to overcome a "visible but controllable threat," eventually the threat will transform itself into an "apparent and uncontrollable threat" (Phase 4). On entering this phase, it becomes impossible for the business organization to attain its ultimate or important goals and the organization cannot help but face bankruptcy sooner or later.

These four phases are each characterized by the existence of a certain type of danger (Müller, 1984, S. 229 ff.). In Phase 1, a business strategy is endangered (*Strategiekrise*); in Phase 2, profitability of the business is endangered (*Erfolgskrise*); in Phase 3, in addition to profitability, the liquidity of the business is endangered (*Liquiditätskrise*); and in Phase 4, survival is endangered, most probably leading to liquidation of the organization (*Liquidation*). In Phase 1, when a business strategy is endangered, the organization is often hindered from increasing or utilizing business opportunities or advantages such as market share or know-how. In Phase 2, when target achievement opportunities are endangered, the organization finds it difficult to attain its profit/sales targets. In Phase 3, when the liquidity of the business is at risk, the organization's sustainability or survival is endangered. In Phase 4, when the organization's liquidation cannot be avoided, creditors' interests are at risk.

In the past, many researchers have attempted to explain the general mechanism of business crises graphically. Most of them use a four-phased process similar to the one described above.

Figure 1 shows a typical mechanism presented by many researchers, including Dreyer *et al.* (2001, S. 6) and Bilker (2000, S. 28), with some adjustments added by the author.

2.3 *Causes of business crises*

Direct causes of business crises include a critical decrease in earnings and a shortage of current assets in hand. In other words, a deterioration in the profitability and liquidity of the business could directly cause a business crisis, and it is obvious this is the root cause of most business crises.

One detrimental situation involves what is called the "fixed costs problem" (*Fixkostenproblem*). A problem with fixed costs (*fixe Kosten*) results from a specific condition — overcapacity (*Überkapazität*). This condition can be construed as due to an inappropriate relationship between productive capacity and production volume. In short, the fixed costs problem is the result of the following situation:

$$Productive\ capacity\ >\ Production\ volume.$$

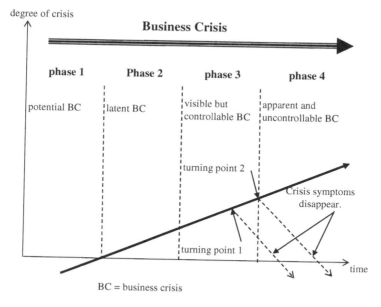

Fig. 1.   Phases of business crisis.
(Adapted and modified from Dreyer *et al.* (2001, p. 6) and Bilker (2000, p. 28).)

Indirect causes can also exist alongside the direct cause. Indirect causes are varied and so are the resulting impacts. Past studies on business crises have been unsuccessful in clarifying the distinction between direct causes and indirect causes. In fact, in past discussions on the causes of business crises and bankruptcies, there was no mention about a direct cause; and only the indirect causes were pointed out.

3   Business Crisis Management

3.1   *Business crisis and business crisis management*

The idea of business crisis management originated in the world of politics. In 1962, the Cuban Missile Crisis acted as a trigger for government institutions worldwide to ponder about the management of such a predicament. In those days, crisis management was construed as a process of making decisions to get through a crisis. It was not until the 1970s that the idea of crisis management penetrated the business world.

To businesses, crisis management means a set of countermeasures against threats to their business activities. Such countermeasures consist of efforts to "avoid" or "overcome" the crisis. As described earlier, a business crisis can be defined as a situation that impedes the achievement of ultimate or important corporate goals or threatens the survival of the business. Therefore business crisis management refers to efforts to detect, understand, avoid, or overcome the said impediment or threat. In a broad sense, "business crisis" covers all four of the previously described threats (potential threats, latent threats, visible but controllable threats, and apparent and uncontrollable threats).

According to Krystek, business crisis management can be categorized into two main types: "active business crisis management" (*aktives Krisenmanagement*) and "reactive business crisis management" (*reaktives Krisenmanagement*). He further subdivides the active category into "preemptive business crisis management" (*antizipatives Krisenmanagement*) and "preventive business crisis management" (*präventives Krisenmanagement*), and the reactive category into "repulsive business crisis management" (*repulsives Krisenmanagement*) and "liquidation business crisis management" (*liquidatives Krisenmanagement*). Then he correlates these four types with the said four threats (Krystek, 1987, S. 105 ff.; Krystek, 1980, S. 63 ff.; Dreyer *et al.* 2001, S. 27 f.), as shown below.

(1) Active business crisis management

    (a) Preemptive business crisis management→potential threats.
    (b) Preventive business crisis management→latent threats.

(2) Reactive crisis management

    (c) Repulsive business crisis management→visible but controllable threats.
    (d) Liquidation business crisis management→apparent and uncontrollable threats.

Preemptive business crisis management constitutes countermeasures against any potential threats (to business strategies), and (in a narrow sense) is a strategic approach. Its objective is to protect the business from any impediments to target achievement opportunities, and also to eliminate such impediments. Specific measures might take the form of (a) withdrawal from those products/markets that are too weak to make the business secure or that could endanger the survival of the business ("withdrawal strategy," which often involves a decision to reduce production capacity); (b) efforts to improve through market penetration or cost reductions to enhance existing business activities and make them secure ("continuation strategy"); or

(c) the launch of any promising product or entry into any promising market through a diversification approach, partnership or acquisition ("aggressive strategy" or "structural conversion strategy"). Thus, preemptive business crisis management presents diverse possibilities.

Preventive business crisis management aims to secure target achievement opportunities by counteracting any latent threat (to target achievement opportunities). Its primary objective is to avoid any impediment to profit/sales target achievement opportunities, but when it seems impossible to avoid such impediment, it becomes necessary to introduce measures to improve profitability that would ensure the sustainability of the business. At the same time, any financial loss or lost profit-making opportunities should be compensated for. When a threat to target achievement opportunities exists, it is necessary to pursue cost reductions in all departments, including production, marketing, research and development, and control/accounting systems and also introduce measures to stimulate demand.

Repulsive crisis management constitutes countermeasures against any visible but controllable threat (to target achievement opportunities and to the liquidity of the business). Its objective is not only to secure target achievement opportunities but also to ensure the liquidity of the business, which is a requisite for the survival of the business. In other words, business crisis management in this phase aims to prevent excessive debts and insolvency. Efforts to avoid bankruptcy are important basically, but even when bankruptcy seems unavoidable, it is necessary to prepare for rehabilitation. Excessive debts or insolvency do not necessarily eliminate all chances of survival and rehabilitation.

Liquidation business crisis management constitutes countermeasures against any apparent and uncontrollable threat (liquidation), and is conducted within bankruptcy procedures. In other words, this business crisis management is conducted in anticipation of liquidation. Figure 2 shows the relationship between a business crisis and business crisis management.

3.2 *Business crisis management and risk management*

Business crisis management and risk management are often confused. This confusion comes from the diversity of possible interpretations for the term "risk" (*Risiko*) and the idea of risk management, and the difficulty in giving clear definitions for these terms.

Many researchers have attempted to explain risk from the viewpoint of "probability" and "the scale of loss" (Burger and Buchhart, 2002, S. 162; Schmitz and Wehlheim, 2006, S. 81 ff.; Yoshikawa 2007, p. 187). In this

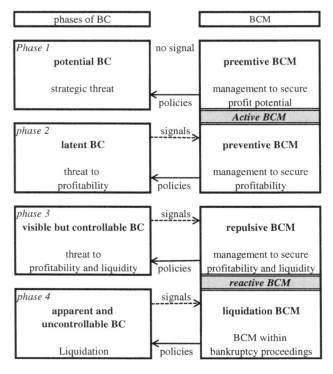

BC=business crisis
BCM=business crisis management

Fig. 2.   BC and BCM.

approach, risk can be defined as the combination of "likelihood of suffering a loss" and "estimated amount of loss." In short, risk can be considered
as "expectable loss." Accordingly, risk management can be defined as measures to reduce risk through efforts to decrease the probability of suffering a
loss and to minimize any loss. Here, the idea of risk is always accompanied
by the assumption of probability (Yoneyama, 2008, p. 17), and therefore a
discussion of risk management cannot be separated from a discussion of probability. This means that the subject of management in "risk management" is
something that will happen in the future (future crisis). In this aspect, risk
management is totally different from business crisis management.

    Basically, the subject of management in "business crisis management" is
any existing threat to a business, and business crisis management requires an

understanding of the causes and effects behind the threat. In this light, the best definition of business crisis management is "counteraction against any visible threats." Also, even when an existing threat shows no explicit visible symptoms, it is business crisis management, not risk management, that is the appropriate term for countermeasures against such a threat.

Then, the question is whether it is business crisis management or risk management that is appropriate in managing a potential threat (in other words, a threat to business strategies). A "potential threat" means that it is before an outbreak, and for this reason, it seems that risk management (rather than crisis management) is appropriate for such a threat. However, it is important to understand the difference between "possible threats," which may or may not invite an outbreak, and "potential threats," which would definitely invite an outbreak if no preventive action is taken. Although they are similar in the aspect of being currently invisible, the significance is completely different between the two. These two threats should be differentiated from one another. Especially, the latter can be considered to be a crisis because its outbreak can be assumed, meaning that a conceivable root cause and an expectable effects exist.

Thus, it is obvious that the subject of management in "risk management" is something that may or may not invite an outbreak. On the other hand, the subject of management in "business crisis management" includes something that would most probably invite an outbreak, as well as latent threats and visible threats. Thus, it is the subject of management that matters. For an understanding of the difference between risk management and business crisis management, it is necessary to think about whether management of your threat requires an analysis of probability or an analysis of the conceivable root cause and expected effects.

4   Conclusions

I explained business crisis management by defining a crisis as "mismanagement at a turning point," and focused on the fixed costs problem in order to establish a logical analysis of business crises. As I mentioned earlier, it was not until the late 1970s in Germany that the significance of business crisis management came to be recognized as a result of serious financial difficulties disturbing business there.

Behind any business crisis, there are direct causes and indirect causes, and the latter can be segmented into exogenous causes and endogenous counterparts. Direct causes include declining profits, a suffered loss, and tight funds. This deterioration in profitability and liquidity are, in most cases, caused by the fixed costs problem. It is important to understand this mechanism to establish a logical and systematized analysis of crisis management.

A business crisis represents a turning point, in which chance and danger coexist, and in this light, a business crisis is an ambiguous phenomenon. Successful management of a business crisis would make it possible to create an opportunity for future development. In other words, appropriate decision making, efficient integration of countermeasures, and restructuring efforts could make sustainable business development possible. Herein lies the paradox inheres in the phenomenon of a business crisis. It is important to be aware of this paradox when discussing business crisis management.

References

Apitz, K. (1987). *Konflikte, Krisen, Katastrophen*, Wiesbaden: FAZ/Gabler Frannkfurt am Main (in German).

Bergauer, A. (2003). *Führen aus der Unternemenskrisen*, Wiesbaden: Erich Schmidt Verlag (in German).

Bilker, K. (2000). Unternehmenskrise, in Bilker K. and Pepels W. (Hrsg.), *Handbuch Krisenbewusstes Management*, Berlin: Cornelsen, pp. 12–24 (in German).

Brühl, V. (2004). Restrukturierung, in Brühl V. and Göpfel B. (Hersg.), *Unternehmensrestrukturierung*, Stuttgart: Schäfer-Poeschel, pp. 3–11 (in German).

Burger, A. and Buchhart, A. (2002). *Risikocontrolling*, München Wien: Oldenboulg (in German).

Dreyer, A., Dreyer, D. and Obieglo, D. (2001). *Krisenmangement in Tourismus*, München Wien, Oldenbourg (in German).

Linde, F. (1987). *Krisenmanagement in der Unternehmung*, Berlin, Akademische Abhandlungen zu den Wirtschaftswissenschaften (in German).

KfW Bankgruppe (2005). *Krisenmanagement*, 2. Aufl., Frankfurt am Main, Frankfuter Allgemeine Buch (in German).

Krystek, U. (1980). Organisatorischen Möglichkeiten des Krisenmanagement, *ZfO*, 49 Jg., 63–71 (in German).

Krystek, U. (1987). *Unternehmungskrisen*, Wiesbaden: Gabler (in German).

Krystek, U. (2006). Krisenarten und Krisenursachen, in Hutschenreuter, T. und Griess-Nega, T. (Hrsg.), *Krisenmanagement*, Wiesbaden: Gabler, pp. 41–66 (in German).

Miyama, A. (2010). *Unternehmenskrise und Management*, Tokyo: Moriyama-shoten (in Japanese).

Müller, R. (1982). *Krisenmanagement in der Unternehmung*, Frankfurt am Main: Peterlang (in German).

Müller, R. (1984). Krisenmanagement als organisatorisches Gestaltungsproblem, *ZfO*, 53 Jg., 229–237 (in German).

Saynisch, M. (1994). Krisenmanagement, in Gareis R. (Hrsg.), *Erfolgsfaktor Krise*, Wien: Signum-Verlag, pp. 49–73 (in German).

Schmitz, T. and Wehlheim, M. (2006), *Risikomanagement*, Stuttgart: Kohlhammer (in German).

Schreyögg, G. (2004). Krisenmanagement, in Heinzen, M. und Kurschwizt, L. (Hrsg.), *Unternehmen in der Krise*, Berlin: Dunker & Humblot, pp. 13–32 (in German).

Yoneyama, T. (2008). *Introduction to Risk and Insurance: Let's Learn from Stories*, Tokyo: Nihonkeizaishinbunsha (in Japanese).

Yoshikawa, K. (2007). *Business Risk Management*, Tokyo: Chuokeizei-sha (in Japanese).

7

Profit Management Model to Overcome the Enterprise Crisis

Noriyuki Imai

Meijo University

1   Introduction

Today, within an increasingly globalized economy, many Japanese enterprises repeatedly find themselves in crisis because of rapidly fluctuating exchange rates. In the mid-1990s, Toyota, one of Japan's leading corporate groups, constructed its "double standard model" of profit management in order to deal with the sharp appreciation of the yen.

In this model, the planning division at the head office first formulates two types of profit plans: one based on general benchmarks and the other based on conservative benchmarks. The profit plan based on conservative benchmarks is then distributed from the head office planning division to be used throughout the company. Subsequently, the company as a whole sets a shared goal to exceed (achieve beyond) the conservative profit benchmarks described in the model.

In profit planning, the negative impact on the profits of rapidly fluctuating exchange rates was conventionally considered to be "beyond the scope of anticipation." However, Toyota's goal with this model was to consider these fluctuations beforehand, put them "within the scope of anticipation" and thereby incorporate them into the initial stage of profit planning. In this way, Toyota aimed to evolve into an enterprise with organizational strength capable of withstanding any crisis caused by rapidly fluctuating exchange rates.

In this chapter, I generalize this model from the perspective of enterprise crisis management and advocate the concept of "crisis boundary management." This concept refers to the conversion of factors that have conventionally been considered beyond the scope of anticipation to within this scope. In addition, the term "Toyota" in this chapter represents the Toyota Group in general; it does not correspond to any individual company within the group.

2   Japanese Enterprises and Globalization

We are living in an era of increasing economic globalization. Because of the advance in telecommunication technologies, the immediate availability of information, and the development of a distribution infrastructure, economic activities such as production, distribution, and consumption are transcending national boundaries and developing on a global scale.

Economic globalization has its origins in the age of geographical discovery. It developed with the rise of capitalism during the Industrial Revolution and then became a full-fledged phenomenon after World War II with the rapid growth of multinational companies. The term "globalization" was first used in the 1960s, but its widespread use only came about following the end of the Cold War in the 1990s, with subsequent expansion of free trade areas (Iyotani, 2002).

Because of economic globalization, product and service transactions from trade have increased; capital, including direct investment, and the labor force have been mobilized on an international scale; distribution networks have developed because of the expansion of air and sea routes; the international financial system has developed; the volume of data in circulation that transcends national boundaries has grown because of the use of internet technology and other factors and global standards for technical standards; and management styles have increased in number. Because of these and other factors, national and regional boundaries have become less relevant, as regional economies have been integrated into the global economy, and enterprises and other organizations throughout the world have deepened their mutual ties.

Amid such economic globalization, multinational firms have grown by striving to optimize their activities on a global scale; that is, they have aimed to globally optimize the various elements of their operations, such as researching technologies, developing products, procuring materials and parts, securing a labor force, accumulating production technologies and capabilities, utilizing a distribution infrastructure, responding to market and customer needs, and complying with standards in various countries. "Global supply chain management" is an example of this as it aims to achieve globally optimized levels of procurement, production, and sales.

In the 1980s, Japan advocated a type of internationalization, where the importance of creating mutual ties with other nations was realized. Then, at the beginning of the 1990s, this idea developed into the notion of a borderless planet, as it seemed that national boundaries had begun to disappear. Subsequently, the above-described concept of globalization became accepted within Japan (Mamiya, 2000). In conjunction with these evolving concepts, the activities of Japanese enterprises also became increasingly globalized.

In the first phase of Japan's globalization, their focus was on the overseas export of domestic products. This played an enormously successful role in supporting Japan's rapid economic growth after World War II. But then Japan gradually overtook U.S. in terms of industrial competitiveness. This provided the backdrop to the intensification in trade friction that emerged between the two nations in the mid-1980s.

The second phase of their globalization was centered on the relocation of procurement and production bases from Japan to overseas. Because Japanese enterprises have been able to maintain their production superiority in quality and productivity, this strategy has achieved certain success up to now.

In the third and current phase, in addition to operational functions such as procurement, production, and sales, the globalization of management as a whole has been rapidly progressing, including core elements such as planning, development, human resources and finances.

Such globalization of economic and corporate activities is creating and maintaining a large range of complementary beneficial functions; for example, improvements in production efficiency through the international division of labor and the use of optimal production sites, better returns on investment through a greater number of choices and increased opportunities to develop technologies made possible by exchanges of personnel and expertise.

In contrast to such benefits, globalization can also have harmful effects. In conjunction with the development of the international financial system and the immediate availability of information, the rapid fluctuation of exchange rates, including the ones due to inflow and outflow of short-term speculative funds, can have a reverse function of backfiring to economic and corporate activities with a negative impact. This point will be considered in further detail below.

3 Exchange Rate Fluctuations and Enterprise Crisis

Today, within an increasingly globalized economy, many Japanese enterprises repeatedly find themselves in crisis because of rapidly fluctuating exchange rates.

The backdrop to this problem is the adoption of the floating exchange rate regime. In contrast to a fixed exchange rate regime, in a floating exchange rate regime, the exchange rate, which is the rate of conversion between currencies, is not pegged at a fixed level, but rather is determined by supply and demand conditions in foreign exchange markets.

Analyzing how the yen–dollar rate has fluctuated since the adoption of the floating exchange rate regime, at the end of 1976, the rate was 300 yen to the dollar. However, by the latter half of 1978, the yen had dramatically appreciated to around 180 yen to the dollar. Prior to the Plaza Accord in 1985, the yen–dollar rate was around 250 yen to the dollar. The yen then rapidly appreciated because of adjustments to exchange rates following the enactment of the Plaza Accord. By the end of 1986, it was 160 yen to the dollar, and by the end of 1988, it had strengthened further to around 120 yen to the dollar. In addition, at the start of 1990, the yen had weakened somewhat to 150 yen to the dollar. However, following the economic bubble in Japan and the subsequent aftereffects, the yen trended at a constantly strong level and continued to set record highs against the dollar, appreciating as far as 80 yen to the dollar by April 1995. Next, the yen–dollar rate went through a period of repeated up-and-down fluctuations. However, against the backdrop of the deterioration of U.S.' twin deficits and the Lehman Shock in 2009, which had its epicenter in the U.S., the fundamental keynote in the dollar–yen rate has subsequently continued to be a strong yen and a weak dollar.

Such a rapid appreciation of the yen against the dollar has plunged the many Japanese enterprises that have developed their business activities globally into crisis. These companies have used trade to increase product sales and services and improved their percentage of sales and profits provided from overseas through direct investment. As a result, even if they implement measures to mitigate the impact of exchange rate fluctuations, in the majority of cases, they will still have significant exchange rate exposure. Therefore, the rapid appreciation of the yen against the dollar, in some cases, has such a negative impact on profits that even the sustainability of some of these Japanese enterprises is threatened.

4 Enterprise Crises at Toyota

In consideration with Secs. 2 and 3, we will now analyze the case study of Toyota, one of Japan's leading corporate groups.

Toyota's founding father, Sakichi Toyoda, was born in 1867. As the predecessor business to Toyota, he established a company to develop and sell automated looms. In particular, he completed the development of the Toyoda Model G Automatic Loom in 1924, which incorporated the principle of *jidoka* (autonomous automation, which means that the machine stops itself when a problem occurs). This principle comprised part of the Toyota Production System introduced in later years.

Kiichiro Toyoda, the founder's son, was born in 1894. Following trips to Europe and the U.S. to observe conditions in their automobile industry, in 1929, he sold the patent for the automatic loom to a British company, and then from 1930, began research on a small gasoline engine. In 1936, he introduced a passenger car, the Toyoda Model AA Sedan. In 1937, he established Toyota Motor Co., Ltd, which began mass production of automobiles in 1938.

By 1950, however, Toyota was experiencing a business crisis. The company went through industrial disputes and had to reduce its workforce. However, it was able to rebuild its business because of the full-fledged launch of the "Just-in-Time" concept within the Toyota Production System.

In 1955, it launched the Toyopet Crown passenger vehicle, and in 1957, the Crown became the first Japanese passenger vehicle exported to the U.S. In the same year, it established Toyota Motor Sales, USA, Inc. (TMS). In 1959, the company began production at Toyota do Brasil Ltda. (TDB) in Brazil. From 1960 onward, Toyota developed its business globally and achieved rapid growth.

By 1986, Toyota, Japan, had produced a cumulative total of 50 million vehicles, a total that increased to 100 million units by 1999. In addition, by 1985, the company had exported a total of 20 million vehicles from Japan to other countries; moreover, by 2002, it had produced a total of 10 million vehicles in North America.

Today, Toyota is one of Japan's leading multinational groups. It currently has 50 production companies in 26 countries other than Japan and has vehicle sales in more than 170 countries. Since its establishment, Toyota has faced varied crises. However, the most serious has been the widely fluctuating exchange rates, specifically the rapid appreciation of the yen against the dollar.

The background to the crises resulting from the rapid appreciation of the yen against the dollar is as previously stated — i.e., Toyota has a significant exchange rate exposure because of the global development of its business. For example, in 2010, Toyota produced approximately 3.3 million vehicles in Japan, but of this number, only about 1.6 million were sold in Japan; the remaining 1.7 million were exported overseas.

In addition, in 2010, Toyota produced approximately 4.3 million vehicles at its overseas production sites. The company requires that a certain level of parts be supplied to these sites from Japan. So Toyota's exchange rate exposure has been trending steadily upward, as not only does it produce vehicles in Japan for export overseas, but also an increasing number of the parts that it uses at its overseas production sites are supplied from Japan. (The same trend can be seen among other Japanese companies in the automobile industry.)

Against this backdrop, on two occasions, Toyota has faced a major crisis because of the rapid appreciation of the yen against the dollar.

The first crisis occurred from 1985 to 1988, when the yen rapidly strengthened against the dollar following the previously described exchange rate adjustments carried out as part of the Plaza Accord. To deal with this crisis, Toyota formed a committee to decide on emergency measures to deal with the strong yen. On the basis of a group-wide horizontal system of cooperation, it formulated and implemented several measures to reduce costs, strengthen its cost planning activities by standardizing units and parts, expand its overseas production sites, and increase their production capacities. As a result of these measures, it was able to avoid falling into deficit in its periodic income.

The second crisis it faced was from 1990 to 1995, when the yen strengthened to around 80 yen to the dollar. As previously described, this was due to the effects of the Japanese economic bubble and its subsequent collapse. To deal with this crisis, Toyota once again formed a committee to decide on emergency measures for the strong yen. The company created a group-wide horizontal system of cooperation to implement various measures to drastically reduce its expenditure and capital investment, to revise the sales price of some vehicles (price hikes), and to revise the parts' procurement prices from some of its suppliers (price cuts). Once again, these measures enabled Toyota to avoid falling into deficit in its periodic income.

However, as the underlying trend in the dollar–yen rate is a strengthening yen and weakening dollar, it is highly likely that in the future, Toyota will face the same type of crisis again. It will not change its basic strategies of strengthening its cost competitiveness and management foundations to deal with this trend. However, in order to deal with rapidly fluctuating exchange rates — specifically, the rapid appreciation of the yen against the dollar — a recognition emerged within Toyota during the times of crisis that it somehow needed to reform its management system in order to maintain its tenability as an enterprise.

The "double standard model" of profit management described below is a management system that developed out of this recognition.

5 'Double Standard Model' of Profit Management

In the mid-1990s, Toyota, one of Japan's leading corporate groups, constructed its "double standard model" of profit management in order to deal with the sharp appreciation of the yen.

In this model, the planning division at the head office first formulates two types of profit plans: one based on general benchmarks and the other based on conservative benchmarks. The profit plan based on the conservative benchmarks is then disseminated from the head office planning division throughout the company. Subsequently, the company as a whole sets a shared goal to exceed (achieve beyond) the conservative profit benchmarks described in the model.

In general, the following six factors are the main drivers of periodic income in the automobile industry:

1. The number of vehicles produced and sold.
2. The model mix of vehicles sold (percentage of sales according to models and specifications).
3. The exchange rate averaged across the period.
4. The amount saved through cost reductions (the amount saved from value engineering (VE) through cost planning activities, the amount saved from value analysis (VA) through cost improvement activities and the amount saved from reductions in part prices from suppliers).
5. Revisions to vehicle sales prices.
6. Fixed costs (labor, depreciation, research and development, sales and distribution) and other costs.

In the past, Toyota's usual method of formulating a profit plan was for the planning division at the head office and the business and function divisions to discuss benchmark values for these six drivers of periodic income. Then, on the basis of the benchmarks they agreed on, the head office planning division created a profit plan, which they disseminated across the entire company, and the benchmarks within it became the earnings targets for the entire company.

However, when using a profit plan based on these types of generalized benchmarks in terms of company management and administration, it was impossible for Toyota to respond sufficiently to the type of exchange rate fluctuations — namely the rapid appreciation of the yen against the dollar — that were discussed earlier.

In other words, in the event of the rapid appreciation of the yen during a certain period, an event that was considered to be beyond the scope of anticipation, a monetary amount corresponding to the extent of the change in the period-averaged exchange rate and the accumulated exchange rate exposure would be generated. This amount would be deducted from the generalized benchmarks in the profit plan.

As a consequence, Toyota would need to revise (hike) the prices of the vehicles it exports from Japan in order to mitigate the actual impact that this deduction amount would have on the periodic income.

However, such price hikes reduce Toyota's relative competitiveness and result in decreasing demand (fall in sales) in the countries to which it exports vehicles, and cause the model mix for its vehicle sales to deteriorate.

In addition, a rapidly appreciating yen has an adverse impact on the Japanese economy. This creates the possibility that demand in Japan for Toyota's vehicles will decline (sales will fall) and its model mix for its vehicle sales will deteriorate.

Therefore, in order to mitigate, even if only to a small extent, the actual impact of this reduction amount on its periodic income, Toyota aims to increase the amount it can save from cost-price reductions by reducing fixed and other costs. However, the main source of savings from cost reductions is the amount saved from VE through cost-planning activities, where in a majority of cases, the savings are first realized through changes to the vehicles' composite parts and unit designs. Therefore, the savings normally require a certain period before they are achieved. Also, even if Toyota is able to convince suppliers to revise their prices for the parts they provide, apart from the case of a short-term price adjustment, in a majority of cases, a certain period will be needed before these revisions can be achieved, as Toyota will have to formulate a fundamental reform plan in cooperation with the supplier.

In addition, there is a limit to the extent that a reduction in fixed costs, such as those for labor, depreciation, research and development, and sales and distribution, can mitigate the actual impact on periodic income, because such cost reductions are intrinsically downwardly rigid.

Toyota created the "double standard model" of profit planning in order to overcome such limitations imposed by the use of generalized benchmarks in profit planning.

Under the "double standard model," as with the conventional method of formulating a profit plan that Toyota had previously used, first, the planning division at its head office as well as the business and functional divisions discuss benchmark values for the six drivers of periodic income. Then, on the basis of the benchmarks they agree on, the head office planning division creates a profit plan.

Next, within the agreed upon benchmarks, the head office planning division estimates the initial level of risk for the period-averaged exchange rate, and then amends it to the most conservative (strong-yen) level possible. It then provisionally calculates the resulting revisions to the sales prices of vehicles (price hikes), the decrease in vehicle sales, and the deterioration in the model mix (percentage of sales according to models and specifications). Then, in addition to setting new conservative benchmarks for each item, it calculates the amount by which periodic income will be reduced on the basis of these benchmarks.

Then, the amount by which the periodic income would be reduced is distributed across the accumulated savings from cost-price reductions (the amount saved from VA through cost improvement activities) and from fixed and other cost reductions. The conservative benchmarks are re-established for each item.

The profit plan based on the conservative benchmarks created by this process is then disseminated by the head office planning division across the company, and a shared goal for the entire company is set to exceed these profit benchmarks. In other words, at the point the conservative benchmarks are first established, they include estimates for the period-averaged exchange rate (a strong-yen level), for revisions to the sales prices of vehicles (price hikes), for a decrease in vehicle sales, and for a deterioration in the model mix (percentage of sales according to model and specifications).

If these risks do not occur during the period, then a decrease in the periodic income because of these factors will not occur.

In this scenario, only the remaining conservative estimates will occur — namely the accumulated saving from cost-price reductions (the amount saved from VA through cost improvement activities) and fixed and other cost reductions — and the conservative profit benchmarks within the profit plan will be exceeded (overachievement).

The objective of the "double standard model" of profit management is to perceive in advance the factors that have conventionally been considered to be beyond the scope of anticipation in profit management — namely the negative impact on profits of rapidly fluctuating exchange rates — and thereby place them within this scope. By incorporating exchange rate estimates into the initial stage of profit planning, Toyota aimed to evolve into an enterprise with organizational strength capable of withstanding any crisis caused by rapidly fluctuating exchange rates.

In other words, if the rapid fluctuation in exchange rates — in particular, the crisis caused by the rapid appreciation of the yen against the dollar — is placed within the scope of anticipation, then at all times, Toyota will have in place conservative benchmarks for sales-related items such as the number of vehicles sold, the model mix for vehicles sold (percentage of sales according to models and specifications), the period-averaged exchange rate, and revisions to vehicle sale prices. It shares these benchmarks throughout the company, and as a result, company employees are constantly being trained in achieving cost competitiveness by reducing the cost price and fixed and other costs, serving to forge a strengthened organizational character. This is where the inherent importance and significance of the "double standard model" of profit management can be found.

6 "Crisis Boundary Management" Concept

The "double standard model" was discussed earlier in this chapter as a profit management model to overcome an enterprise crisis.

Next, from the perspective of the management of an enterprise crisis, I generalize this model to advocate a model of "crisis boundary management" that converts a crisis that is considered to be beyond the scope of anticipation into one that is within this scope.

As previously stated, Toyota's objective for its "double standard model" of profit management was to perceive in advance a factor that had conventionally been considered to be beyond the scope of anticipation in profit management — namely the negative impact on profits of rapidly fluctuating exchange rates — and thereby place it within this scope. By incorporating exchange rate estimates into the initial stage of profit planning, Toyota aimed to evolve into an enterprise with organizational strength capable of withstanding any crisis caused by rapidly fluctuating exchange rates.

The key point here is to perceive in advance a crisis that had been considered to be beyond the scope of anticipation, and thereby convert it to being within this scope. So, how do we perceive a crisis before it actually occurs?

In general, the control theory consists of two control methods: feedback controls and feedforward controls.

The traditional feedback control method involves returning to the input side the outcome of a controlled output, comparing it to the benchmark values, and then attempting to use it in the next controls. The feedback controls are adjusted after the outcome of the provided manipulated variable is observed. With this method, if external factors that disturb the controls (disturbances) occur suddenly, it is not possible to make adjustments until after these effects manifest themselves.

Feedforward controls were created to deal with this issue. With feedforward controls, when an external factor (disturbance) that has an effect on the output occurs, the necessary adjustment operations are carried out beforehand in order to minimize this effect as much as possible. Because feedforward controls adjust before the effects of an external disturbance manifest themselves, it is necessary to decide on the methods to be used to detect these external factors (disturbances) and the manipulated variable to be used when external factors (disturbances) are being detected.

From the perspective of an enterprise's crisis management, the indication of superiority as a control method of feedforward controls over feedback controls is redundant. Even the previously discussed "double standard model" is basically an example of a management system based on the feedforward control way of thinking. However, the question that needs to be answered here is, "How do we maintain in place a method of detecting external factors (disturbances), such as an enterprise crisis?"

In order to detect an external factor (disturbance) such as an enterprise crisis — or in other words, to convert a factor considered to be beyond the scope of anticipation to one within this scope prior to its occurrence — the size of the domain that consists of crises that are beyond the scope of anticipation must be reduced as much as possible. Conversely, the size of the domain that consists of crises that are within this scope must be made as large as possible.

On this point, Simons (1994) has provided a useful suggestion. He stated that, in order to successfully execute a strategy, four key elements must be analyzed and understood: core values, risks to be avoided, critical performance variables, and strategic uncertainties. Each of these elements is controlled by the following four levers of control, which are systems with different objectives.

1. Belief Systems: Systems used to encourage the search for new opportunities and provide direction for this search.
2. Boundary Systems: Systems used to define the boundaries of the search for opportunities.
3. Diagnostic Control Systems: Systems used to provide a motivation to achieve a specific goal, to monitor the progress toward achieving it, and to provide compensation commensurate with the progress made in achieving it.
4. Interactive Control Systems: Systems used to promote learning within the organization and thereby help creating new ideas and strategies.

Simons noted on one of the levers of control, "boundary systems," that, on the basis of clearly recognized business risk, these systems limit the search for opportunities and define the boundaries for actions that may be taken by a member of an organization.

Based on this, Simons suggests that the concept of boundaries and their setting and control is an important factor. In other words, from the perspective of risk management, he seems to state that while boundaries are established to limit the actions that a member of an organization may carry out, the corporate body must control these boundaries in a direction where the domain to perceive business risk can be maximized.

On the basis of this consideration, in order to perceive a crisis before it occurs and thereby move it from being beyond the scope of anticipation to within this scope, an essential requirement seems to be identifying the boundaries that separate what can be anticipated from what cannot be anticipated, and setting control boundaries in order to maximize the size of the domain that is considered to be within the scope of anticipation.

Considering such implications, this chapter advocates the concept of "crisis boundary management" as a method by which enterprises can manage a crisis by perceiving it before it occurs, and moving it from beyond the scope of anticipation to within this scope.

7 Conclusion

Since the end of the 20th century, the financial world has undergone several rapid developments on a global scale, including the globalization of the financial and capital markets, the liberalization of finance and the easing of restrictions, the shift from indirect financing to direct financing, the accumulation of private-sector capital that has accompanied economic growth, the growth in the scale of financial and capital markets, the rise of institutional investors, and the "informatization" of the financial sector.

In conjunction with these developments in the international financial system and the immediate availability of information within it, the rapid fluctuations in exchange rates, including the short-term flow of speculative funds into and out of the foreign exchange markets, has meant that economic globalization is increasingly causing a negative effect on the activities of enterprises.

Recognizing this situation, this chapter considers an enterprise crisis management perspective to discuss the "double standard model" of profit management as a means by which enterprises can overcome a crisis. In addition, I generalize from the enterprise crisis management perspective found within this model and advocate the concept of "crisis boundary management," which signifies moving a crisis that has conventionally been considered to be beyond the scope of anticipation to one within this scope.

The business environment for enterprises in the 21st century is continually evolving because of economic globalization. In conjunction with this evolution, it is highly likely that enterprises will increasingly face crises caused by rapidly fluctuating exchange rates. In such an environment, it can be considered that the "double standard model" of profit management and the "crisis boundary management" that is advocated in this chapter will assume increasing relevance.

References

Iyotani, T. (2002). *What is Globalization? Reading and Understanding a Liquidizing World*, TYO: Heibonsha (in Japanese).

Mamiya, Y. (2000) "Globalization and Creating Public Spaces", in *Japan's Concept in 2025*, Yamaguchi, Y. and Kamino, N. (eds.), TYO: Iwanami Shoten (in Japanese).

Simons, R. (1994). *Levers of Control: How Managers Use Innovative Control Systems to Drive Strategic Renewal*, MA: Harvard Business School Press.

PART 4

Supply-Chain Management after the Disasters and TPS after Business Crisis

8

Robust Supply-Chain Management for the Disasters: Based on the Product Design Architectures

Yasuhiro Monden
University of Tsukuba

Rolf G Larsson
Lund University

1 Introduction: Theme of This Chapter

The Just-in-Time production system, or lean production system, tries to achieve a continuous flow of production, thereby reducing the inventories of materials, works-in-process, and finished products. As a result, only minimum levels of inventories exist in the various layers of the supply chain. Under this situation, the major earthquake followed by the tsunami that on March 11, 2011 in Eastern Japan affected many parts manufactures when they were hit by these disasters. And since there were only limited buffer inventory due to JIT systems, many major Japanese manufacturing companies suffered from a shutdown of its supply chain.

This leads to the theme of this chapter, how could we reinforce the JIT production system for the whole supply-chain *not to stop their flow of parts* due to disasters that stop production at partial locations in the chain? The authors will explore the approach of achieving a continuous flow of production rather than stockpiling the inventory in order to have a robust supply chain.

2 Conceptual Framework of Robust Hybrid Supply Chain

2.1 *Two concepts of product composition: Specialized parts and common parts*

From the viewpoint of product design architecture there are two concepts of parts (Fujimoto, 2002 and 2004):

(A) Group of specialized exclusive-use parts for a specific model of a certain company, which is called an "Integral" type. The example is a kind of specific part to be utilized only in the car-model B (such as the hybrid car of *Prius*) of Toyota Motor.

(B) Group of common parts (commonly usable parts, standard parts), which is called a "modular" type. For example, a printer of various printer-makers can be utilized for a certain company's personal computer system such as Dell (for modularity, see Baldwin and Clark, 1997; Aoki and Ando, 2002; Baldwin, 2002; Fujimoto, 2002 and 2004.)

Thus any products, whether it is an automobile or a digital electronics product, is composed of the above (A)-type parts (integral-type parts) and (B)-type parts (modular-type parts). For the production of these different parts, it would be useful to identify patterns of Hybrid Products that have varied proportions of these two different kinds of parts, in order to consider the product design strategy or to construct a solid supply chain. In this chapter, we will label the completed output at each layer as Product and the "input" items that will be directly imbedded into this output is called Parts.

2.2 *Hybrid supply chain that uses both market and network organization*

Based on the two concepts of product design architecture described above, four types of parts can be classified:

(1) **"Closed" Custom Parts Suppliers from Network**
    Custom-made specialized part for use by the specific model of a specific assembler, supplied from Keiretsu.[1]

---

[1]The *Keiretsu* is a group of firms that are formed and controlled by a core company and has a long-term transaction relationship with the core company. They are allied with the core company in terms of capital ownership, managerial directors, or inter-firm transaction, etc.

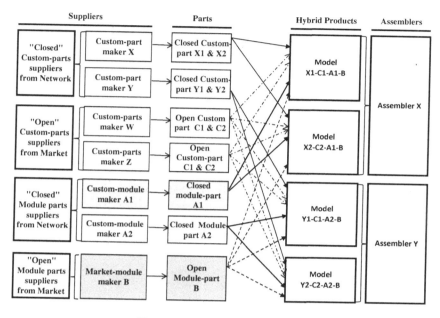

Fig. 1.   Hybrid supply chain.

(2) **"Open" Custom Parts Suppliers from Market**
Custom-made specialized part for use by the specific model of a specific assembler, supplied from market.

(3) **"Closed" Module-parts Suppliers from Network**
Custom-made common modular part for use by the various models of a specific assembler, supplied from Keiretsu.

(4) **"Open" Module-parts Suppliers from Market**
Common modular-part for use by various models of various assemblers, supplied from the market.

The authors' proposition in this chapter is that the hybrid supply chain has all of these four types at the same time, which is composed of (1) custom parts from the network, (2) custom parts from the market, (3) custom module parts from the network, and (4) common module parts from the network (see Fig. 1).

The example of (2) "open" custom parts for use by the specific model of a specific assembler, supplied from market, is shown by the smartphone of Apple's iPhone 5. The iPhone 5 uses the custom-made "liquid crystal display" (LCD panel) called the "retina display," and this panel is supplied by the suppliers of Japan Display (Japan), Sharp (Japan), and LG

Display (Korea), which are competing in the market. Note, also, there are many models of the smartphone made by Samsung Electronics, Sony Mobile Communications and Sharp, etc. in the market, and each of them has its one custom-made panel.

2.3　*Cost-reduction efficiency versus attractiveness by differentiation*

The modular-based parts are usually good for cost-reduction efficiency, since they can enjoy both scale-merit and scope-merit, thanks to the wider use of these parts in a variety of models. The specialized parts have a benefit of differentiating the products for competitiveness, since they can add the special attractiveness to individual customer's preferences.

Therefore, as the authors see it, the mixture of larger use of modular-based parts and the less but effective use of specialized parts could yield both efficiency and attractiveness.

Robust supply chain by modules

When the ratio of the group of common basic parts to all of the parts become larger (that is, if the proportion of common parts become larger than the proportion of specialized parts), then the safety or robustness of supply chain can be enhanced. There are two reasons for this:

(1) The scale merit can be enjoyed by the common-module supplier who can enhance their capacity-usage rate and reduce costs; thereby they can spread their plants in many locations on account of the increased order volume and profits they earned.

(2) When common parts are used by the assembler, various parts suppliers who have so far been producing various custom-made parts will also make the common part in question, and the number of regional locations of the common part plants will increase. However, when the common parts are introduced by the assembler, the number of various kinds of parts will also be reduced, and thereby some part suppliers may be superfluous and removed from the assembler's network.

2.4　*Development stages of modular parts*

Two development stages of modular parts are identified as follows (Fujimoto, 2002 and 2004):

Stage #1: The parts commonly used among various models of *a certain firm*. An example is the common "platform" of Toyota that may be commonly used for model X and model Y, but it will not be used by any other auto maker.

Stage #2: The parts commonly used among various models of *the industry*. Such common parts can be utilized by rival automakers. Examples of such parts include the motor of *Mabuchi* and the CPUs of *Intel*. Mabuchi Motors in Japan supplies power windows, door locks, head lights and electric parking brakes, etc. to many auto makers in Japan. Mabuchi uses their *"de fact"* standard sub-parts built on their own technology. This approach may be a prospective direction for Japanese parts suppliers who have competitive technology just like the CPU of Intel.

Even if a common part at Stage #1 is used only within Toyota, for instance, it gives the part maker the merits of mass production compared to the custom-made parts. Then it could be economically easier for the part maker to diversify the locations of their manufacturing plants. In case that industry-wide common parts at Stage #2 would be more widely used in the auto-industry, or bike-industry, the inter-network of the supply chain would be more solid. Then the JIT philosophy could be established even when disasters occur.

3 Modular Design Architectures at Volvo and Ikea, as Evidence of the Robust Hybrid Supply Chain

3.1 *Volvo global architecture*

After Volvo had sold its private car section to Ford in 1999, later acquired by Geely, there remains what is called Volvo Commercial Vehicles, hence referred to as Volvo.[2] Its activities are divided into nine business areas: four different truck areas, buses, construction equipment, boat engines, aircraft engines, and financial services. For providing support to these areas, there are five business units: Volvo 3P, Volvo Powertrain, Volvo Parts, Volvo Logistics, and Volvo IT. Together, the business areas and units form a matrix organization (see Fig. 2).

---

[2]If nothing else is stated, quotations, facts and figures are taken from Volvo's internal publications and from the Volvo homepage, http://www.volvo.com/. In a major dynamic consortium like Volvo facts keep changing all the time. The data presented here was available in June 2012. Background data of Volvo and Ikea also comes from Anderson and Harsson (2006).

| Volvo | Trucks | | | | Volvo Buses | Construction Equipment | Volvo Penta | Volvo Aero | Volvo Finance |
	Volvo	Renault	Mack	"Asia"					
3P									
Power train									
Parts									
Logistics									
IT									

Fig. 2.   Volvo's matrix organization.

(Annual Report, 2011, p. 94 quoted from http://www.volvo.com/)

Volvo 3P coordinates product planning, product development, and purchases for the four truck companies. Powertrain (engines, gearboxes, and axle shafts) is the world's greatest manufacturer of diesel engines, with a cylinder volume of more than 8 L. Powertrain supplies the entire group with engines and drive train gear, including gearboxes, axle shafts, and other components. Volvo Parts is responsible both for purchases and for the product development of parts for the entire group. Volvo Logistics develops and manages logistics solutions for the automotive and aerospace industries worldwide. Volvo IT provides the whole group with complete business-supporting IT solutions.

To illustrate the modular design in the matrix, we will focus on Volvo Construction Equipment and its best-selling product, the Articulated Hauler, a huge dump truck for conveying rocks, debris, etc. A frame-steering articulated hauler basically consists of two parts: a front with engine, gearbox, axle shafts, wheels, and cabin. The rear contains another frame with axle shafts, wheels, and a body with a hydraulic lift. The front and back frames are connected by a hydraulic frame-steering mechanism which is unique to Volvo's Articulated Hauler (Volvo Art). The company sometimes compares its haulers to a Tyrannosaurus Rex on wheels. An articulated hauler can make its way nearly everywhere. Volvo Art produces about 2500 articulated haulers per year. The total cost model below shows the modules concerned (see Fig. 3).

Module	Price	Supplier	Comments
Engine	xxx xxx	Volvo	Core module
Cab	xxx xxx	Volvo	Core module
Transmission	xxx xxx	Volvo	Core module
Tires etc	xxx xxx	Other	Global purchasing
Other materials	xx xxx	Other	Global purchasing
Value adding	150 000		Own activities
Administration	50 000		Own activities

Fig. 3.   Module costing for an articulated hauler.

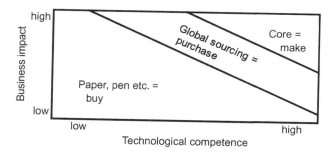

Fig. 4. Strategic Make or Buy matrix for Volvo Art.

More than half the value is supplied by Volvo. The strategically important parts are bought from Volvo Powertrain[3] and Volvo Parts, and other material like tires, hubs, etc. from other suppliers. Volvo's strategic purchasing model involving global purchases is followed. The administrative costs also include development and other costs. The manufacturing is computerized and robotized to a very high degree.

Volvo Art is an industrial company comprising many different areas of technology. The various modules, parts, and details required can be manufactured by Volvo Art, some other Volvo company, or an external business. The choice of production is controlled by strategic considerations made by Volvo Art together with Volvo, on the basis of a so-called strategic matrix (see Fig. 4). This is a way of trying to maintain the core competences they want to keep within Volvo.

With the help of the strategic matrix, Volvo Art can decide when running its own production is appropriate and when to buy from sub-suppliers. The top right corner of Fig. 4 shows the core activities run by Volvo. They comprise engines, transmissions, axle shafts, and certain parts. For Volvo Art, the core activities consist of robot-welded bodies and frames for articulated haulers. The Global sourcing square stands for advanced procurement. It includes parts or services which make great demands on technological knowledge and whose business impact

---

[3]As indicated in Fig. 1, Volvo Powertrain delivers modules of engines and transmission to all Volvo Construction Equipments, such as the Articulated Haulers. The seven different Volvo Articulated Hauler models, from A25E to A40E, are built on four modules of engines and transmissions. These modules are shared with other Construction Equipments like wheel loaders and excavators.

is great.[4] Some examples of purchased parts are tires and wheels from Michelin and others. The company has chosen to call it "purchase" to distinguish this form of procurement from less complicated buying, of pens and paper, for instance. Buying of this type is found in the bottom left corner of the matrix.

In purchasing, Volvo tries to find suppliers who can cope with "completed" or "partly completed products" in the words of the purchasing manager. One aim is to get finished products or modules to the assembly lines. This means that all pre-assembling is outsourced. Volvo Art has over 200 suppliers. These suppliers are evaluated according to a manual, the Supplier Evaluation Model for the Volvo Group. The purpose of having a common model is making an evaluation of current and new suppliers on the basis of a common procedure for all Volvo enterprises, providing supplier information, in the form of both functional and technical data, and increasing the knowledge about each supplier. In this way, the common model is intended to be an aid in developing suppliers and facilitating the fact-related purchase decision process as well as permitting a continuous follow-up process. Much of this material can also be found on Volvo's homepage, so that any potential suppliers know what will be required of them.

Robust supply chain management at Volvo

The modular design at Volvo is used at all appropriate levels, from purchased sub-parts at Volvo CE to the matrix of the whole Volvo Group. Modularization is the basis that enables Volvo to continue to invest in the common modules in their core competence of Powertrain and Parts and purchase other modules from their strategic partners. All the common modules and parts are manufactured in multiple global Volvo plants. All purchased modules and parts come from competitive suppliers spread over the three continents Asia, Europe, and the Americas as a way of spreading risks for disasters.

Attractiveness and cost efficiency of Volvo

A Volvo Articulated Hauler is designed to give its customers, in different types of construction businesses, the lowest possible cost per ton of load, which is the basis of Volvo Art's competitiveness. The "rough"

---

[4]The advanced procurement is made from Volvo's strategic partners on long-term transaction contracts. These partners comprise what could be described as Volvo's network organization.

attractiveness of the Tyrannosaurus Rex-like design indicates robustness. The hardware is complemented with a vast net of services, like maintenance and financial services. Volvo uses its own versions of target costing and value engineering. Following the target cost strategy, all costs are "designed" with the appropriate Volvo modules. The modular design of all Volvo's differentiated products is a basis for cost efficiency. The total cost for an Articulated Hauler is shown in the module costing table. By using more than 50% common modules, Volvo enhances capacity-usage and scale economy which reduces costs. Manufacturing is computerized and robotized to a very high degree, which also implies a very good cost control and efficiency. With the help from the strategic matrix for Volvo Art, they can decide to buy non-core products and parts globally.

3.2 *Ikea global architecture*

The history of Ikea is synonymous with that of Ingvar Kamprad, the entrepreneur. He was born in 1926 and grew up on the farm of Elmtaryd in the parish of Agunnaryd in Sweden. These four names form the acronym of IKEA, the company he started in 1943.[5] During the first decade, Ikea was a small local furniture business. In 1955, Ikea decided to design their own furniture and to deliver the products in flat packages, two decisions that proved to be successful. Through design, Ikea gained control over the entire value-creating process. The flat packages contributed to low cost for internal transport, processing, transport damage, storage, and to the customers themselves, adding to value by home transport and assembly.

Porter (1996) described Ikea's links between activities and strategy as a fundamental element of competitive strength (see Fig. 5). Strategic positioning means that a company performs other activities than its competitors or does so in a different way. *"The essence of strategy is choosing what not to do"* (Porter, 1996, p. 70). An activity map shows how the strategy is upheld by a number of tailor-made activities. Strategy, according to Porter, is about achieving harmony among company activities.[6] In the Ikea activity map presented in Fig. 5, the dark circles indicate

---

[5]Unless otherwise stated, quotations, facts, and figures are taken from Ikea's internal publications and from Ikea's homepage http://www.ikea.com/.
[6]The self-selection, self-transport, and self-assembly is attractive to Ikea's customers, as it involves the customer in the process of improving his home and living at the same time as it saves costs and thereby the price of the modular furniture.

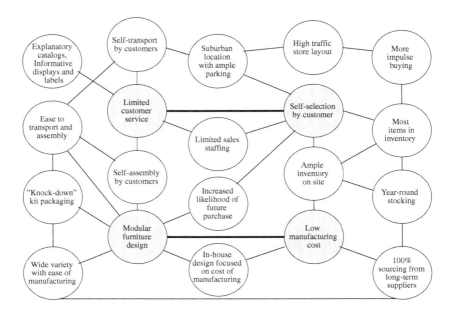

Fig. 5.   Ikea activity map.

(Porter, 1996, p. 71.)

Ikea of Sweden	Kitchen	Storing	Sleeping	Seating	Children	Textile	etc...
Wood							
Board							
Metal							
Plastic							
Components							
etc...							

Fig. 6.   Ikea of Sweden's matrix organization (Internal material).

the top-priority strategic elements, which are implemented by related activity groups marked by light circles.

Combining its own product range with its own modular furniture design, flat packages, coordinated purchases and catch-your-breath pricing are the strategic elements assigning Ikea's special role in the value.

The Ikea concept is controlled by Ikea of Sweden, which can be described as the heart of the organization. Their operation is carried out in a matrix form of departments, like kitchen and storing, and materials like wood and board. In Fig. 6, the departments on the horizontal axis are "joined together" by the material specialists on the vertical axis system.

To describe the modular furniture design in the matrix, we will focus on one of the typical Ikea products "Billy the bookshelf," one of the company's best-selling products. Billy comes in about a thousand variants, but the combinations consist of a few modules. Billy is a part of the storing department, is built on board and uses, as all Ikea furniture, modular components to assembly the bookshelf in the customer's home. Some of the modules of Billy are shared with some in Kitchen, Sleeping, and Children's department.

The majority of Billys is manufactured by Swedwood, Ikea's production company. At its global plants, Swedwood produces modular furniture in massive wood and flat furniture of board, as Billy. Over the years, Swedwood has acquired a world-class production capacity. Before the establishment of Swedwood in 1992, Ikea purchased all its furniture from global suppliers. To continue the partnerships with these suppliers, Ikea decided to put a ceiling for Swedwood's production at 10% of Ikea's total purchase value. This limitation has proven to be of great value to Ikea, who is satisfied with its mix of own production and other partner suppliers in a robust supply chain.

Purchasing decisions are strategically important, and to support these decisions, Ikea has developed a purchasing matrix (see Fig. 7). By means of the matrix, an overview is obtained of alternative geographical locations. For each material concerned, the attractiveness of the regions has priority. The matrix is updated twice a year. Apart from material supply, the priorities are based on factors like the national rate of growth, risk-taking, and the UN sanction lists. The basic rule for purchasing is, as always, best buy. With the matrix, Ikea is updated with global market prices and conditions, which is an essential part of the strategic cost accounting at Ikea and for its cost leadership strategy.

The choice of a supplier must be satisfactory from both the supply and the distribution point of view. It is essential to be able to effectively

Ikea purchasing matrix	Ceramics	Glass	Natural fibres	Lighting	etc...
Qingdao	▓		▓		
Shanghai				▓	
Taiwan					
Vietnam	▓			▓	
Malaysia			▓		
Indonesia				▓	
Thailand	▓				
Laos	▓				
Bangladesh	▓				

Fig. 7. Ikea's purchasing matrix.

transport raw material and components between various processing steps and from then on to the global Ikea warehouses.

Robust supply chain management at Ikea

The modular design of the Ikea furniture and the use of Swedwood for some of the development and manufacturing give Ikea a reliable supply chain. Before the introduction of Swedwood, Ikea could not secure deliveries to all its stores. Now they have the option to manufacture on its own if other suppliers fail to deliver. The modular design and the flat packages are two of Ikea's core competences that enable them to manufacture their furniture in multiple global plants spread over the world. With the help of the purchasing matrix, Ikea manages the robustness of the supply chain and spreads the risks for disasters.

Attractiveness and cost efficiency of Ikea

The attractiveness and competitiveness of Ikea comes from the unique mix of activities in the Ikea activity map. The modular design of furniture is a basis for Ikea's cost leadership. Ikea uses target costing for all its furniture, and the first they design is the price-tag. Price minus margin gives target cost. All prices are fixed for a year, as in the Ikea catalog, which forces Ikea to try to have production cost fixed for the same period. Ikea aims at prices at least 20% lower than competitors, which means that total cost also have to be at least 20% lower. Following the target cost strategy, all costs are "designed" with the modular furniture by value engineering, including design for flat package. With the knowledge from the purchasing matrix, Ikea can chose to buy products and parts globally depending on market conditions. If Ikea is unable to reach target cost for a product, an assignation is made to Swedwood for *kaizen*-costing for lower manufacturing costs.

4   Modular Design Architectures at Toyota and Nissan, as Evidence of the Robust Hybrid Supply Chain

4.1   *Toyota new global architecture*

Toyota's new development method called *Toyota New Global Architecture* (TNGA) first prepared three core platforms (chassis)[7] for FF (front-engine,

---

[7] "Platform" concept: The term "platform" originally stands for the chassis of automobile. It means the whole running function mechanism that includes basic frame, engine, mission, accelerator, brakes, etc. This terminology is based on the

front drive) car series (*The Nikkei*, 24 November 2011; 2 March 2012; 10 April 2012; Toyota (2012). The three platforms are

(1) Platform for compact *Corolla* class,
(2) Platform for compact *Vits* class, and
(3) Platform for middle *Camry* class.

Each of these core platforms is commonly used by multiple car series, which will further use common components or common modular parts. However, the strategic parts that relate to exterior and interior (trim) designs will be differentiated depending on the regional conditions and tastes. Note that the exterior and interior parts are visible for the customers, while components of the platform are invisible for the customers.

These three platforms will cover about 50% of total number of produced units of Toyota cars. The above technique is summarized in Fig. 8:

The effects of this parts commonization will be:

(1) 20% reduction in the manufacturing costs: By this effect, Toyota tries to yield profits in the emerging countries with lower-price cars (i.e., increase of the return on sales in the emerging countries).

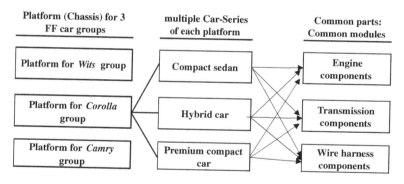

Fig. 8.   Toyota's new development method called TNGA.

(Adapted and modified from *The Nikkei*, 10 April 2012.)

product design architecture for the passenger cars of 50~60 years ago and for even the middle or big class Commercial vehicles such as trucks of the current days, which have the architecture of the so-called "Body-on-frame" type, in which the frame-structure (chassis) has the running function mechanism by itself, and on this frame the body will be installed. On the other hand, since the modern passenger cars have the architecture of the so-called "Monocoque" type (or "*frameless construction*"), where the whole body itself has both frame and body as a unified structure, the term chassis or platform nowadays roughly implies the underbody portion as a running functional mechanism.

(2) 30% reduction in development staff number and development time (by the end of 2012 compared to 2009): In other words, both development labor costs and development lead-time will be reduced by 30%.

(3) The reduced amount of costs and workforce can be moved to efforts for product differentiation and thus to enforcement of merchandize power for each customer and region. This may avoid the situation that the competitive power of merchandize might be weakened by common parts application.

(4) Reduction of the number of outsourced parts from the previous 4000~5000 items to 2000~2500 items (i.e., half of the parts will be commonized).

As a result, the remarkable reduction in number of auto-parts suppliers will happen and therefore the remaining part manufactures will get orders for larger volumes of common parts with a request to reduce costs based on the scale merit. Further, because of reduction in the number of suppliers, alliances or merger and acquisitions will be accelerated.

Effects on the changes in supply chain at Toyota

Since the common modules in Fig. 8 are merely the common parts within Toyota Motors, they are custom-made parts for Toyota only. Therefore they are not *open* common modules for all of the automobile makers at this stage of modularization, thus the automakers must compete in the market using the modules differentiated among automakers.

Further, since each automaker will buy such *closed* modular parts from the specific part-makers, the suppliers' network will still continue to exist rather than the competitive market of suppliers.

Notwithstanding such limitations, because the number of parts items will decrease and the production volumes of the common parts will become larger, such parts makers can spread their locations of plants on account of the enlarged economic ability. As a result, the supply chain can be spread, which makes it more robust to big disasters.

4.2 Nissan's common module family

Nissan also used to prepare the specific platform (chassis) for each specific size of cars, and the common parts were used for the same platform, thereby the number of parts items was reduced and thus manufacturing costs were reduced. This is based on the same idea as Toyota's TNGA as described above.

However, Nissan decided to introduce a new designing technique called the *Common Module Family* (CMF) from the new models to be sold after 2013. First, regarding the automobile structure, each of the following four structural-components (mechanisms) will have common modules for multiple types of cars. These modules will be differentiated depending on the varied heights and weights of each structural-component. The structural-components are:

(1) Engine compartment (mechanism surrounding the engine and transmission, etc.).
(2) Cockpit (mechanism surrounding the panel of electronic measurement instruments).
(3) Front-underbody (mechanism surrounding the front wheels including the suspension).
(4) Rear-underbody (mechanism surrounding the rear wheels that supports the car weight).

For these four structural-components, the following modules will be prepared:

(1) There are two modules for engine compartments in terms of height: high hood and low hood.
(2) There are three modules for cockpit in terms of position: high, middle, and low positions.
(3) There are three modules for front-underbody in terms of weight: heavy, middle, and light weights
(4) There are three modules for rear-underbody in terms of weight: heavy, middle, and light weights

Any car will be classified as belonging to a certain "Family Group" in terms of similarity in the mixture of height and weight, and thus the cars of the same Family Group will use the same modules for each of their four structural-components. The image of such a relationship between the Family Groups and the structural-component modules will be visually depicted as in Fig. 9.

Take Mini-van (MPV) and Sport-utility vehicle (SUV), for example. These two cars will be grouped as being able to use the common module of the engine compartment, since both cars have high bonnets for their engines compartments.

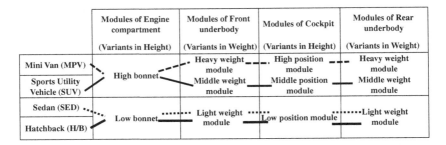

Fig. 9.   Nissan's common module family.

(Adapted from Nissan motors news-release on 27 February 2012.)

Further, both Sedan (SED) and Hatchback (H/B) are equally low in their engine compartments and cockpits, and are also equally having light weight in their front- and rear-underbody, thus SED and H/B can use the common modules of these structural-components.

Actually, in addition to the above four modules, Nissan also has another module for the structural-component called "Electronic Architecture," which comprises various electronics parts, such that Nissan's CMF is also called the "4 + 1 Big module concept."

It seems apparent that Nissan's CMF is somewhat different from Toyota's way of utilizing common modules from the viewpoint of platform differences. As we see it, however, both approaches are essentially similar, since Nissan also use the same modules of the structural-components depending on the difference in the size of cars (i.e., difference in weight and height).

Effects on the changes in supply chain at Nissan

Nissan raises the following merits as the effects of the Common Module Family (*The Nikkei*, 2012, Feb. 28):

(1) Reduction in the development costs by 27%.

(2) Ratio of Design commonization will be enhanced up to the 80% from the current 40%. Among the total number of production units, the adoption ratio of CMF will be 12% in 2013, but its adoption rate will be increased up to 58% in 2016.

(3) It is expected that the manufacturing cost can also be remarkably reduced in addition to the development cost reduction, on account of increase in the ratio of design commonization. This is because of enhancement of capacity-usage ratio of facilities in the parts makers such that the scale economy could be enjoyed.

5 Conclusion: Summary of Case Comparisons and our Suggestion for Optimal Balance of Hybrid Supply Chain

5.1 *Summary of case comparisons*

If we compare the four cases, it is obvious that the four companies, all in their own way, work with modular designs. But it is also clear that Volvo CE and Ikea have a longer history of modularization, for Ikea more than 50 years. Table 1 presents a summary of findings of modular design and management of supply chains in the four cases (see Table 1).

What we have seen so far is mostly evidence of modules in stage 1, where the four case companies work with firm-specific modules. In other words, both Toyota and Nissan are using the firm-specific modules of the structural components depending on the platform differences in the size of cars. Also Volvo, with its Matrix organization, and Ikea, with its Activity map, work with firm-specific modules.

However, we have seen some examples from Volvo and Ikea, where they take steps toward some usage of modules common for the whole industry. In the Module costing example from Volvo, we find a mixture of stages 1 and 2, with a majority of inter-firm Volvo modules like Powertrain and Cab, but also the module Tires and Wheels that is an example of a stage-2 common industry module (Michelin and others). In the Ikea of Sweden matrix, we found that some modules in the beds, from the sleeping/metal matrix, were sourced from common industry module makers (Hilding Anders).

These two examples show that hybrids of stage 1 and stage 2 modules exist. The Volvo Strategic Make or Buy matrix (Fig. 4) indicates, with its span of "Global sourcing," that the border of the "Core = make" corner can be altered. It is possible to keep the Volvo Art brand with even more modules coming from stage 2 common industry module suppliers. If the development of common industry modules continues into more of stage 2, there is a great possibility of improved cost efficiency.

So far, the Japanese automobile industry has been exercising their competence on account of sharing the parts development information via the design of simultaneous engineering between auto-maker and parts maker, through the *keiretsu* network (i.e., allied relations between both parties). However, after the auto-maker's expansion of the common modular parts, they will proceed to more "global purchasing" beyond the existing *keiretsu* network. Actually, the Japanese auto-makers' global purchasing

Table 1.   Case comparisons.

Cases / Criterions	Toyota	Nissan	Volvo	Ikea
Integral Design	Tailor-made parts for Toyota	Tailor-made parts for Nissan	Tailor-made parts for Volvo	Self-selection of various modules by customer
Firm specific modular design (stage 1)	TNGA (Toyota New Global Architecture)	NCM (Nissan Common Module Family)	Volvo Matrix Organization	Ikea Matrix Organization
Industry common modular design (stage 2)	Global sourcing beyond Keiretsu network	Global sourcing beyond Keiretsu network	Global sourcing by "Make or Buy matrix"	Global sourcing by "Purchasing matrix"
Robust supply chain	Mixture of modular parts of both stage 1 and 2	Mixture of modular parts of both stage 1 and 2	Mixture of modular parts of both stage 1 and 2	Mixture of modular parts of both stage 1 and 2
Cost efficiency	Mixture of modular parts of both stage 1 and 2	Mixture of modular parts of both stage 1 and 2	Mixture of modular parts of both stage 1 and 2	Mixture of modular parts of both stage 1 and 2
Attractiveness by differentiation	Tailor-made parts for Toyota	Tailor-made parts for Nissan	Tailor-made parts for Volvo	Self-selection of various modules by customer

has accelerated recently, while the Japanese part makers must also increase to sell their produced parts to the customers beyond the assemblers within the *keiretsu* network. Further, the global alliances of parts suppliers through M & A are increasing (*The Nikkei*, 10 April 2012).

We have noted that the case organizations are working toward the Hybrid Supply Chain. In this process, make or buy decisions are of strategic importance, and all case companies work with supplier networks to get a robust supply chain.

Evidence from the four case companies show that they have been continuously working with cost efficiency. We noted that cost reduction is important in all the activities performed in the companies, from the early phases of new product development, to searching for suppliers of common modules and into manufacturing. Target costing is a common tool for all cases.

5.2 Optimal balance of hybrid supply chain that comprises cost efficiency and attractiveness

The essence of our proposition in this presentation lies in Fig. 1, where Hybrid Supply Chains have the four kind of parts from mixed uses of Network and Market. Whether the supply chain will move to the market-like mechanism or to the network-like organization will depend on the proportion of the parts type that dominates the product structure. "The strategy should follow the environmental change." Thus, for the selection (strategy) of the product design structure, the company should also consider the viewpoint of building the solid supply chain to cope with the big disasters (environment), as well as the market differences (another environment).

In order to determine the mixed use of the four kind of parts, the top management should find the Pareto Optimum Points of the Hybrid Products composed of four types of parts. In other words, the optimal balance among the following four different types of parts in Fig. 1 can be selected according to the concept of Pareto optimum, which will be explained in the following paragraphs.

Two goals of the hybrid products

Goal 1 of the custom-made parts for each model of each car maker is the attractiveness in terms of differentiation. Goal 2 of the "open" modular parts for various car-makers of the car industry is the efficiency in terms of cost reduction, while the "closed" modular parts for various models of each car maker and the "open" custom-made parts of each model of each car-maker have the feature in the middle of the above two types of parts, that they simultaneously have both goal 1 of Efficiency and goal 2 of Attractiveness.

However, since any manufacturer (assembler) tries to have a mixture of the above four types of parts and form the hybrid supply chain as depicted in Fig. 1, the assembler usually wish to achieve a compromise of both goal 1 and goal 2. It will be easier to understand their preferences if we would classify the markets into three categories:

(a) Market for the less wealthy customers, where majority of the people prefer the efficient models.
(b) Market for the wealthy customers, where majority of the people prefer the attractive models.
(c) Market for the middle class customers, where majority of the people prefer both efficient and attractive features.

Multiple Pareto Optimum Points

Multiple Pareto Optimum Points may be found as a set (called Frontier) of the non-dominant solutions (also called the non-inferior solutions or the *efficient* solution). The top management can apply the utility function that reflects their priority reach the two goals, and get the unique solution point for allocating the investment fund to the four different parts.

Let us see the graphical exhibition for the multiple Pareto optimal balances of parts mixture and how the unique optimal balance could be determined. We take the dimension of Efficiency in the vertical axis and the dimension of Attractiveness in the horizontal axis (see Fig. 10). The Pareto optimal point stands for the allocation of resources where if another allocation is selected for improving the goal 1, the other goal 2 will be worsened. On the other hand, if some change of the current resource allocation will improve both goals 1 and 2 at the same time, then the Pareto optimum is not yet achieved and the "Pareto improvement" could still be available.

Utility function as the trade-off ratio between efficiency and attractiveness

For a certain manager, the set of mixture of Efficiency and Attractiveness that gives this manager an equivalent amount of utility is called the "utility function" as an indifference curve. The utility function will actually have a concave form, since any utility function is subject to the law of diminishing marginal utility. Such utility function will move to northeast in the two-dimensional graph of Efficiency and Attractiveness when the utility is improved.

A certain investor (top management or CEO) may think that if the goal 1 (i.e., Efficiency) is *a little* reduced the goal 2 (i.e., Attractiveness) must be *largely* improved in order for his or her utility to be equal between before and after. This is the utility function (a) of the investor who invests for the less wealthy customers. On the other hand, the utility function (b) of the investor who invests for the wealthy customer would be seen in the situation where if the goal 2 (i.e., Attractiveness) is *a little* reduced the goal 1 (i.e., Efficiency) must be *largely* improved.

Determination of the unique optimal balance between efficiency and attractiveness

The unique optimal balance between the Efficiency goal and the Attractiveness goal will be determined at the contact point of both Frontier curve of Fig. 10 and Utility function. This was shown in Fig. 11. In the figure, the utility function that reflects the trade-off ratio (c) corresponds to the manager who will produce and sell the products to the majority people of the middle class customers.

Thus the points a, b, and c correspond to the optimal balance points for the less wealthy customers, the wealthy customer, and the middle class customers, respectively. And each optimal balance point has its own optimal supply-chains. Among three different forms of the supply chain, the point "a" will make the *strongest* supply-chain for the disasters, and the point

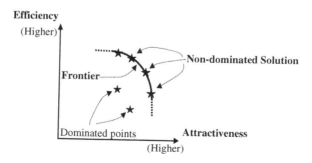

Fig. 10.   Multiple Pareto optimum points on the frontier.

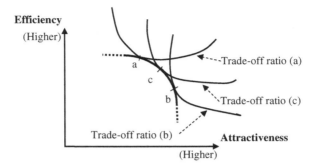

Fig. 11.   Optimal balance between efficiency and attractiveness.

"b" will make the *weakest* supply-chain under the disasters in terms of least use of common parts, while the point "c" will be in the middle.

If we take the automobile company for instance, the Japanese mini-car manufactures such as Daihatsu and Suzuki will take the strategy of point "a", but the big auto-makers such as Toyota and Nissan will have a so-called full-line strategy and sell their cars to all of the markets "a", "b", and "c" at the same time, and thus they seem to have three types of supply-chains at the same time.

Then for the big automobile manufactures who have full-lines, what kind of overall supply-chain will be built? Is it robust or not as a whole? To this question, we have an idea for an answer. As for the common parts the "same" common parts are used commonly in all markets of (a), (b), and (c), each of which at least partially the common parts are utilized. Thus the supply chain for procuring the common parts will be globally and jointly used by the various products for markets (a), (b), and (c). As a result, the overall supply-chain can also be robust to disasters.

Acknowledgments

One of the co-authors, Monden, is grateful to Prof. Kjell Arvidsson and Prof. Jan Alpenberg of Linnaeus University, Sweden, where he was given a chance of visiting professorship in the fall semester 2011, though the sections on Volvo and Ikea and the comparative analysis were mostly written by Rolf Larsson. Monden's acknowledgment must also go to Mr. Anders Westerberg, Volvo Production System Support, and Mr. Anders Johansson,

Product Platform Articulated Hauler, both belonging to Volvo Construction Equipment.

References

Andersson, G. and Larsson, R. G. (2006). *Boundless Value Creation — Strategic Management Accounting in Value Systems Configuration*, Växjö: Växjö University Press.

Aoki, M. and Ando, H. (2002). *Modularity: Essence of the New Industrial Architecture*, Tokyo: Toyo-Keizai-Shinbun (in Japanese).

Baldwin, C. Y. and Clark, B. (1997). Managing in an Age of Modularity, *Harvard Business Review*, September–October, 84–93.

Baldwin, C. Y. (2002). Cost and value of modularity, in Aoki, M. and Ando, H (eds.) *Modularity: Essence of the New Industrial Architecture*, Tokyo: Toyo-Keizai-Shinbun (in Japanese), pp. 67–96. (This paper is mostly adapted from Baldwin, C.Y. and Clark, B. (2000). *Design Rules: The Power of Modularity*, Vol. 1, Cambridge, MA: MIT Press.)

Fujimoto, T. (2002). Japanese supplier system and modularity: Case study of automobile industry, in Aoki, M. and Ando, H (eds.) *Modularity: Essence of the New Industrial Architecture*, Tokyo: Toyo-Keizai-Shinbun (in Japanese), pp. 169–202 (in Japanese).

Fujimoto, T. (2004). *Philosophy of Japanese Manufacturing*, Tokyo, *Nihon-keizai-shinbun* (in Japanese).

Ikea Homepage. Available at: www.ikea.com. Material from home pages, annual reports, etc.

Nikkei Business (2012). *Indomitable Supply Chain*, No. 1631, March 5 (in Japanese).

Nissan Motors (2012). News release, 27 February. "Nissan will introduce the *Nissan CMF* (4+1 Big module concept), the new technique of car design for the new generation cars." (in Japanese). At: http://www.nissan-global.com/JP/NEWS/2012/_STORY/120227-01-sj.html, accessed February 27, 2012.

Porter, M. E. (1996). What is strategy? *Harvard Business Review*, 74(6), 61–78.

The Nikkei (2011). Toyota steers new course: Global common design of parts. 24 November (in Japanese).

The Nikkei (2012). Nissan will make common designs covering various car types and reduce 27% development costs. 28 February (in Japanese).

The Nikkei (2012). Half reduction of investment through common parts at Toyota within 4 years for enhancement of competitive power. 2 March (in Japanese).

The Nikkei (2012). Toyota will reduce costs by 29% through common platform. 10 April (in Japanese).

Toyota Motor Corporation (2012). Homepage news. Toyota releases the
challenge for the better production method of automobiles. At: http://
www2.toyota.co.jp/jp/news/12/04/nt12_0410.html, Accessed April 9,
2012 (in Japanese).

Volvo Homepage. Available at: www.volvo.com. Material from home pages,
annual reports, etc.

9

Management of Humanitarian Supply Chains in Times of Disaster

Yoshiteru Minagawa
Nagoya Gakuin University

1 Purpose of the Study

Management of humanitarian supply chains in times of disaster facilitates successful planning, implementation, and control of the swift, cost-effective flow of goods and related information, from owners of such supporting resources to vulnerable people affected by the disaster. The main sources of revenue for humanitarian disaster relief chains are government budget and donations from humanitarian aid agencies and individuals. As disasters occur, potential donors such as Governments and the world community are informed on how effectively humanitarian supply chains have deployed disaster relief aid, and they accordingly make a decision on which humanitarian supply chains to donate to. It turns out that participants in a humanitarian supply chain need to work collaboratively toward delivering effective disaster relief aid to encourage donations.

The critical success factors in the management of business supply chains are coordination and cooperation among partners (Xu and Beamon, 2006; Monden, 2010). Since humanitarian disaster relief supply chains are characterized by hastily formed networks, they naturally appear at a glance as being confronted with difficulties in achieving coordination and cooperation. This study sheds light on how to build a powerful humanitarian supply chain capable of further enhancing coordination and cooperation, and thereby strengthening its disaster relief contributions.

Moreover, if a rapid response in the immediate aftermath of disasters fails, saving human lives becomes difficult to achieve. A rapid start-up on actions for saving human lives is a mission of humanitarian supply chains. To achieve this successfully, a humanitarian supply chain is required to achieve self-funding for the rapid start-up. Fundraising for humanitarian relief aid comes from government budgets and donations from humanitarian aid agencies and individuals from around the world. However, these fund sources are irregular, unstable, and uncertain. This study discusses a method of self-funding for rapid response to save human lives, under which respective partners in a humanitarian supply chain determine the amount of contribution they can make according to their own means.

As mentioned earlier, this study examines management practices in humanitarian disaster relief chains to build a humanitarian supply chain that enables further strengthening of its disaster relief contributions. In particular, this study focuses on the partners' respective voluntary fund contributions suitable for the characteristics of humanitarian supply chains.

2   Characteristics of Humanitarian Supply Chains in Times of Disaster

Disaster management encompasses phases both before and after a major emergency. Pre-disaster management is typically sub-divided into two phases: mitigation and preparedness. The mitigation phase involves, for instance, activities to construct robust structures against disasters, such as the building of breakwaters. The preparedness phase includes community education on the actions to reduce disaster risks and the contingency storage of pharmaceutical products and food. *Ex ante* disaster management embraces the objectives of saving human life and rehabilitation (Wassenhove, 2006, pp. 480–481).

Let us now consider the impact of pre-disaster risk reduction activities on saving of human lives, using the concept of quality costing. A managerial implication of the quality costing theory is that investments in preventing the production of products that do not conform to specifications help in reducing the production of poor quality products, consequently decreasing total quality costs. This highlights the importance of pre-disaster risk management in the entire disaster relief cycle.

One noteworthy difference between disaster relief and quality control is that while manufactures can achieve zero-defects, humans can hardly prevent the occurrence of disasters. Furthermore, a failure of the quick-relief response mechanism in the aftermath of the disaster is one of the most critical aspects endangering human life. This implies that humanitarian aid effort focused on post-disaster rapid relief is as important as pre-disaster relief.

This study addresses the ways to enhance the integration of a humanitarian supply chain in the aftermath of disasters. The following discussion provides an analytical comparison of humanitarian and commercial supply chains in terms of objectives to be attained, participating entities, and funding resources.

2.1 *Objectivities*

One significant difference between a commercial and a humanitarian supply chain is that the former is a profit-seeking organization, while the latter is a non-profit one. There are several missions for humanitarian relief networks to achieve in the aftermath of disasters, including the saving of human lives in the location of the disaster, alleviating suffering, and maintaining human dignity (Good Humanitarian Donorship). Actions required of a humanitarian supply chain's participants to achieve these missions include the use of ICT (Information and Communication Technology), intelligence gathering on information, and goods needed by disaster victims, and rapid delivery of relief goods to the disaster victims.

All partners in a humanitarian supply chain participate collaboratively in the network to aid disaster victims. This means that a humanitarian supply chain comprises entities having a common mission to be attained, one of which is the provision of humanitarian disaster relief aid (Fig. 1).

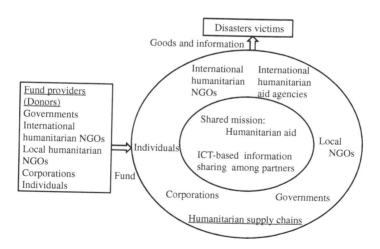

Fig. 1.   Humanitarian supply chains.

Source: Researcher's conceptualization of humanitarian supply chains.

2.2 Participating entities from different sections of business and society

A commercial supply chain essentially consists of for-profit companies. On the other hand, a humanitarian supply chain for disaster aid comprises not only companies but also non-profit organizations. Participants in a humanitarian supply chain are drawn from different communities and come together to engage in humanitarian aid activities. A humanitarian supply chain always involves the United Nations; international humanitarian non-governmental organizations; local non-governmental organizations; governments in disaster-affected countries; and other countries, companies, and individuals.

As mentioned earlier, a company is typically a profit-seeking entity, while on the other hand, humanitarian aid never includes actions motivated by profits, leading us to the following question: what motivates business actors to participate in humanitarian relief actions? According to Thomas and Fritz (2006, p. 116), companies' motivations to participate in humanitarian aid activities include the following aspects: when disasters interrupt the flow of business, companies' participation in relief operations is beneficial in minimizing their own economic loss. In addition, corporate involvement in aid efforts facilitates the demonstration of good corporate citizenship to different stakeholders.

A critical issue of social significance for companies is the achievement of customer satisfaction through supply of goods and services to markets. However, relief from this corporate social responsibility is unfortunately hindered by occurrence of disasters. Companies' collaboration with relief agencies to make efforts for humanitarian aid is beneficial for them to restart delivery of goods to disaster-stricken areas.

2.3 Performance evaluation

Business performance of a commercial supply chain is determined by market response to goods supplied, and in parallel, the market reputation of a business supply chain affects its profitability. With respect to a humanitarian supply chain, its performance evaluation is based on the criterion of whether it has succeeded in effectively saving human life. The international community evaluates humanitarian supply chains. This community reputation of humanitarian relief networks affects the size of budget for disaster relief efforts authorized by governments and the amount of donations received from humanitarian aid agencies and individuals.

2.4 *Fundraising for relief aid operations*

While a major funding resource for commercial supply chains is customers' payment in exchange for goods and services rendered by their business actors, fundraising for humanitarian relief aid comes from government budgets and donations from humanitarian aid agencies and individuals. An important issue regarding funding for humanitarian disaster relief chains is the uncertainty surrounding governments' approval of budgets and humanitarian relief agencies' provision of donations for disaster relief aid. Hence, humanitarian supply chains' funding is typically unstable.

2.5 *Challenge to vulnerable predictability*

Humanitarian supply chains are destined to conduct operations while being relatively more exposed to uncertainty, compared to commercial supply chains. The main objective of humanitarian supply chains, both during and after disasters, is to distribute the required goods and information to disaster-affected residents as quickly as possible. However, humanitarian supply chains in times of disasters are forced to work under unpredictability and uncertainty, as they hardly know what, who, when, and how much to supply. ICT can help humanitarian supply chains in managing uncertainty. This will be detailed in later sections of this study.

3 Management Systems to Facilitate Coordination of Humanitarian Supply Chains

A humanitarian supply chain in times of disasters is typically a hastily formed network. A humanitarian relief network is established by participants from different sections, who are usually working independently in their own areas of expertise and join forces to participate in humanitarian aid in the event of disasters. Hence, disaster relief networks are formed by humanitarian organizations having a shared mission of aiding the disaster-affected in times of disasters. The implementation of effective human life saving and rehabilitation efforts both during and after occurrence of disasters depends largely on whether all of the participants in the hastily formed humanitarian relief network can collaborate and coordinate to achieve their mission (Denning, 2006). A key success factor in supply chain management, regardless of whether it is humanitarian or commercial, is the method to enhance coordination and cooperation among the respective partners (Xu and Beamon, 2006, p. 4; Balcik *et al.*, 2010, p. 24). To do so successfully, several agendas discussed as follows need to be overcome. To increase the overall supply chain profitability, it is imperative to strategically plan, build, and utilize interdependence among participating organizations as well as interaction among operations conducted by different participants. Further, it is important to motivate participants to make managerial decisions leading to an increase in supply chains' total profitability (Xu and Beamon, 2006). As participants in humanitarian supply chains of hastily formed networks in times of disasters are previously working independently in their own areas of expertise before the occurrence of disasters, humanitarian relief networks are forced to face more difficulty in promoting coordination, relative to commercial networks.

The first order of response for participants in humanitarian supply chains in the event of disasters is a network-wide effort to intensify mutual cooperation among participants, based on information-sharing geared toward effective emergency relief efforts.

Denning (2006) introduces the concept of conversation spaces to conduct conceptual analysis on the ways to develop an effective medium for communication in times of disasters. The conversation space involves three factors: physical systems, players, and interaction practices (Denning, 2006, p.17). Using Denning's conversation spaces, two factors facilitating the coordination of humanitarian supply chains are explained as follows.

3.1 *ICT-based networks*

ICT has made remarkable progress in recent years, resulting in the expansion of various types of world-wide communication available, including one-to-one, one-to-many, and many-to-many communication modes (Jaeger *et al.*, 2007, p. 598). Humanitarian supply chains utilize ICT as invisible pipes capable of performing the functions of linkage between humanitarian supply chains and disaster-affected communities. Humanitarian supply chains' mission is the prompt and proper supply of goods and information needed by disaster-affected residents. According to Nishigaki's study on the effects of a network on disaster relief, a communication route is subdivided into an official; top-down; and a private, bottom-up route (Nishigaki, 2011). Gatignon *et al.* (2010) showed that humanitarian aid is better when humanitarian aid organizations are decentralized, through a study on how a humanitarian emergency aid network should be organized. Gatignon *et al.* (2010) have researched disasters-related response efforts led by the International Federation of Red Cross and Red Crescent Societies

(IFRC), having found that IFRC's traditional centralized humanitarian supply chains have transformed into decentralized humanitarian supply chains in the last decade. An analytical comparison of decentralized and centralized humanitarian supply chains will be presented as follows, based on Gatignon *et al.* (2010).

According to Gatignon *et al.* (2010), IFRC was characteristic of a centralized humanitarian supply chain till 2006. How does a centralized humanitarian supply chain deploy relief operations in terms of management of an inter-organizational network? First, IFRC's headquarters are responsible for making almost all decisions on aid operations. The headquarters organized a Field Assessment Coordination Team (FACT) that was sent to disaster-affected areas to assess the needs of beneficiaries (Gatignon *et al.*, 2010, p. 103). FACT delivered information on the needs of beneficiaries solely to the headquarter managers upon return to the headquarters. Apparently, IFRC has traditionally kept information on the needs of beneficiaries under the central control of headquarters, instead of promoting information-sharing among all other participants involved in humanitarian aid efforts. The headquarters, using disaster-related information that was acquired from FACT but was not being updated regularly, have determined a list of goods to be sent to disaster-affected areas and have delivered it to participants engaged in disaster-relief efforts (Gatignon *et al.*, 2010, p. 103). As for how each participating entity decided on what to distribute to disaster areas, each participant individually selected its respective choice of goods from the listed items, as opposed to selecting collectively in a highly coordinated manner (Gatignon *et al.*, 2010, p. 103).

A drawback of the above-mentioned humanitarian supply chain is its ineffectiveness and limited ability to capture the needs of beneficiaries, that is, the way IFRC traditionally acquired information was almost solely through FACT. This possibly hinders current disaster-related, information-based decision-making. Consequently, such centrally controlled decision-making processes could likely give rise to failures such as over-supply of goods to disaster-affected areas and delivering goods that are not needed by beneficiaries. Furthermore, the way in which each participating entity in the IFRC previously determined the goods to supply to disaster-affected areas was autonomous, instead of being based on information-sharing among all participants. As a result, partners often sent the same relief items to the same disaster areas (Gatignon *et al.*, 2010, p. 103).

With respect to a decentralized humanitarian supply chain, its effectiveness stems from its ability to enable coordination based on information sharing among its partners. The key success factor for the prompt distribution of the right relief items to the disaster victims at the right time involves access to the latest disaster-related information, driven by collaborative and cooperative group decision-making on what to send to beneficiaries, where to send the disaster items, and how to send disaster items to beneficiaries. This benefits rapid disaster responses.

As mentioned previously, achieving an increasingly effective humanitarian supply chain requires participants to share information on the extent of damage, location of storage of relief goods, storage quantity, and distribution routes. According to Nishigaki (2011), the internet is based on packet communication characterized as decentralized, bottom-up type communication networks. Thus, the internet facilitates a network connecting humanitarian supply chains and disaster-affected regions.

3.2 *Sharing a common mission among partners*

Key factors for facilitating collaboration and coordination among humanitarian supply chain partners involve a shared mission to exert humanitarian relief efforts. Each participant in a humanitarian supply chain principally collaborates to exert disaster relief efforts for a non-profit purpose. Such an existence of a shared mission is beneficial and supportive to the promotion of coordination in humanitarian relief networks. As mentioned previously, the respective participants in a humanitarian supply chain network are usually working in different sections individually and independently. For the partners to attain an increase in donation through further strengthening of the humanitarian contribution to saving human life, it is imperative to achieve humanitarian supply chains' mission of emergency relief. The goal of building and managing an effective and efficient humanitarian supply chain is to save human lives.

Based on previous studies on supply chain management, one of the most important factors is the attainment of goal-congruence among partners (Minagawa, 2010). A humanitarian supply chain consists of entities that participated in it and work together toward a shared purpose of exertion of disaster relief efforts. Thus, there exists a reasonably unified mission within a humanitarian supply chain. Therefore, despite being characterized as a hastily formed network of disaster relief response in times of disasters, a humanitarian supply chain enables building of trust immediately after launch of relief operations (Tatham and Kovács, 2010, p. 39). This stems from all participants' perception that they belong to a network that is unified by a common goal such as disaster relief.

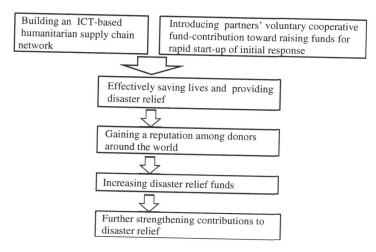

Fig. 2.   A roadmap for further strengthening contributions to disaster relief.

4   Critical Success Factors of Humanitarian Aid Supply Chains

Figure 2 shows a roadmap for the attainment of a sustainable humanitarian supply chain. An explanation for the figure is as follows.

4.1   *Achieving humanitarian aid effectively as well as efficiently, thereby increasing earnings*

As an increase in revenue leads to a company's growth, in the same way humanitarian supply chains' enhanced earnings, such as donations, lead to increased contributions toward disaster relief. A possible way to achieve sustainability in humanitarian supply chains is for them to invest increased earnings in the improvement of emergency relief operations and to capture the fruit of their investment, thereby enhancing their reputation in the international community.

While companies generate sales from providing goods and service to customers, a humanitarian supply chain's funding sources include government subsidies and donations from various humanitarian aid organizations. When donors make a decision on which humanitarian supply chains to donate, they focus on the rule of best value for money. Central to the driving forces for humanitarian supply chains to achieve enhanced reputation in the international community is the attainment of the distribution of the right relief goods to the right beneficiaries, at the right time, in the right quantity.

4.2   *Importance of rapid start-up of initial responses to save human lives*

Here, we focus on saving human lives in the overall humanitarian disaster aid framework. Attainment of this goal requires launching initial rapid response mechanisms to save human lives immediately after the occurrence of a disaster. Rapid start-up of initial responses to saving lives strongly induces donations in the following manner. As disasters occur, potential donors commence a decision-making process on which humanitarian supply chains to donate to. Suppose that a certain humanitarian supply chain promptly launched initial responses to human life saving, during potential donors' engagement in the choice of humanitarian disaster relief chains for donations, and that donors were informed of the humanitarian supply chain's rapid start-up response through media. Such media reports on the humanitarian supply chain's rapid start-up of initial responses enable the humanitarian supply chain to attract donors.

A successful rapid start-up of initial response to saving human lives in a humanitarian supply chain benefits its strengthening of the humanitarian disaster relief contribution. However, humanitarian supply chains are inevitably confronted with an issue of how to fund prompt startup of initial responses, which will be explored subsequently.

4.3   *Usefulness of ICT from the perspective of achieving effective humanitarian disaster relief*

A driving force for a humanitarian supply chain to be highly admired in the international community and thus to attain sustainable funding is the provision of goods and information needed by disaster-affected residents at the right time in the right quantity. Hence, the most effective and efficient disaster relief aid mechanism depends on information-sharing within the entire humanitarian supply chain.

The information that enables humanitarian supply chains to attain rapid and effective delivery of emergency relief goods to disaster-affected residents includes the needs of disaster-affected residents, the location of disaster relief goods, the appropriate route for delivering relief goods to affected areas, and what each partner should deliver. The most important aspect of information-sharing in times of disasters is that in the post-disaster phase, internet enables humanitarian supply chains to connect to disaster-affected areas.

4.4 *Partners' voluntary cooperative fund-contribution according to their respective means for funding quick start-up of initial response*

As previously discussed, pre-disaster responses in the preparation phase are highly subject to unpredictability. That is, before disasters strike, decision-making problems such as what to deliver, quantity of relief goods to be delivered, and where to deliver are characteristics of uncertain challenges.

When unfortunate disasters strike, ICT endows a humanitarian supply chain with a life-safety environment. ICT allows a humanitarian supply chain, in the aftermath of the disaster, to capture the current disaster's situation and to share information with the participants. Furthermore, such ICT-driven information sharing gives rise to effective decentralized approaches to disaster relief. Through synchronizing ICT-based communication with decentralized humanitarian aid, each participant in humanitarian supply chains can effectively and efficiently determine disaster relief planning with the right actions to engage in and when and where to execute them. It turns out that decentralized humanitarian aid aligned with ICT-based communication is able to function as a supportive network for swift response to disasters.

However, any humanitarian supply chain faces uncertainty regarding whether it will succeed in raising funds in the aftermath of the disaster. Notwithstanding the fact that rapid start-up of initial responses to saving human lives is supportive toward the strengthening of disaster relief contributions, humanitarian supply chains are required to resolve the fundraising issue for rapid start-up of initial aid efforts in the early stages of a disaster. An effective way to secure funds for rapid launch of initial responses to save human lives is the application of partners' respective voluntary fund-contribution within their own means, under which the fundraising process proceeds in the following manner.

As a disaster occurs, participants in a humanitarian supply chain collaboratively formulate a plan of initial disaster relief responses, subsequent to making an estimate on the funds required to implement the disaster aid efforts. An effective fundraising method to generate as much aid money as possible is the application of partners' voluntary fund contributions. A key success factor in partners' self-funding lies in the right selection of a method to determine the amount of money funded by respective partners, for which contribution funding should be suitable, given the humanitarian supply chains are not-for-profit organizations. Consequently, it is important to introduce a contribution method under which respective partners voluntarily determine the amount of contribution they can make according to their own means. These funds contributed by partners are characteristic of internal funds of a humanitarian supply chain. A humanitarian supply chain's investment in such a self-funded money mechanism to execute initial disaster responses would result in the achievement of the goal of saving human lives, and potential donors would be informed of this through media, thereby increasing donations to the humanitarian supply chain.

4.5   *Effectiveness of partners' voluntary cooperative self-funding*

The above-mentioned discussion on partners' voluntary cooperative fund contribution provides valuable insights for improving the liquidity profile of partners. Additionally, cost contribution arrangements among partners basically lead to risk-sharing. The partners' voluntary cooperative self-funding mechanism in humanitarian supply chains embraces a risk in that initial disaster relief operations funded by partners' respective fund contributions are not always successful. Such risk-sharing among participants in a humanitarian supply chain is helpful to increase coordination and cooperation among partners from the following perspective.

A key to controlling an inter-organizational network is the management of partners' mutual organizational relationships and coordination of interdependence among actions conducted by each partner. Alternatively, it is important for humanitarian supply chains to create well-coordinated and highly cooperative partnerships conducive to an increase in donations through strengthening humanitarian disaster aid contributions.

As in Simatupang *et al.* (2002, p. 291), coordination among participants in an inter-firm network, including a supply chain, has two analytical perspectives, namely, the mutuality of coordination and the focus of coordination. The mutuality norm in an inter-firm network suggests that partners' collective responsibility toward successfully building a sustainable growing network contributes to stronger and closer relationships among partners (Simatupang *et al.*, 2002, p. 292). Moreover, successful sharing of joint responsibility for increased overall network performance requires diffusion of a common understanding across organizational borders (Simatupang *et al.*, 2002, p. 292). Useful means to generate a common understanding in an inter-firm network include sharing of information and goal-congruence. The focus of coordination covers areas from the activities conducted by each partner to partners' business administration methods (Simatupang *et al.*, 2002, p. 293).

By focusing on the management of humanitarian supply chains, partners' voluntary cooperative fund-contribution for self-funding initial disaster responses promotes risk-sharing as well as joint responsibility for increasing donations.

5 Summary

Previous studies on controlling an inter-firm network show that it is critical to address the enhanced coordination and cooperation among partners in order to establish sustainable and powerful partnerships. Participants in a humanitarian supply chain usually work independently and in the event of a disaster, join forces on efforts to save lives. From this perspective, humanitarian supply chains with a hastily formed network would appear to face significant difficulty in achieving any increase in coordination and cooperation among partners. However, the shared goal of disaster relief activities among partners in the humanitarian supply chain creates the motivation to improve coordination during such times. Moreover, humanitarian supply chains enable the building of an ICT-based network that supports decentralized humanitarian disaster relief contributions. These factors have a significant positive effect on the achievement of enhanced coordination and cooperation among partners in a humanitarian supply chain.

Considering the sources of funding in humanitarian supply chains, to further strengthen disaster relief activities, there is a need to fund a rapid disaster response. Fundraising for humanitarian relief aid comes from government budgets and donations from aid agencies and individuals from around the world, which are irregular, unstable, and uncertain funding sources. Particularly, the method of raising funds for the rapid start-up needed for an initial response to saving lives, poses a significant difficulty for humanitarian supply chains. Humanitarian supply chains most likely depend on self-funding in the early stages of the disaster cycle. This study discusses how each partner builds fund-contributions, on their respective means, to support rapid initial disaster response.

Acknowledgments

I am indebted to Professor Yasuhiro Monden (Tsukuba University), whose comments and suggestions on the appropriate cooperative cost contribution in a humanitarian supply chain have made a significant contribution to my study.

References

Balcik, B., Beamon, B.M., Krejci, C.C., Muramatsu, K.M. and Ramirez, M. (2010). Coordination in humanitarian relief chains: Practices, challenges and opportunities, *International Journal of Production Economics*, 126, 22–34.

Denning, P.J. (2006). Hastily formed networks, *Communication of the ACM*, 49(4), 15–20.

Gatignon, A., Wassenhove, L.N.V. and Charles, A. (2010). The Yogyakarta earthquake: Humanitarian relief through IFRC's decentralized supply chain, *International Journal of Production Economics*, 126, 102–110.

Good Humanitarian Donorship. Available at: http://www.goodhumanitariandonorship.org/. Accessed on April 20, 2012.

Jaeger, P.T., Shneiderman, B., Fleischmann, K.R., Preece, J., Qu, Y. and Wu, P.F. (2007). Community response grids: E-government, social networks, and effective emergency management, *Telecommunications Policy*, 31, 592–604.

Minagawa, Y. (2010). How can management accounting achieve goal congruence among supply chain partners, in Hamada, K. (ed.), *Business Group Management in Japan*, Singapore: World Scientific Pub. Co., pp. 121–136.

Monden, Y. (2010). Concept of incentive price for motivating inter-firm cooperation, in Hamada, K. (ed.), *Business Group Management in Japan*, Singapore: World Scientific Pub. Co., 193–208.

Nishigaki, T. (2011). Decentralized approaches to natural disaster management, *"Economic Column" Series on the Role of Internet-Based Systems in Effective Natural Disaster Management*, May 3, 2011, Nikkei Shimbun.

Simatupang, T.M., Wright, A.C. and Sridharan, R. (2002). The knowledge of coordination for supply chain integration, *Business Process Management Journal*, 8(3), 289–308.

Tatham, P. and Kovács, G. (2010). The application of "swift trust" to Humanitarian Logistics, *International Journal of Production Economics*, 126, 35–45.

Thomas, A. and Fritz, L. (2006). Disaster relief, Inc., *Harvard Business Review,* 84 (November), 114–122.

Wassenhove, L.N.V. (2006). Blackett Memorial Lecture Humanitarian Aid Logistics: Supply Chain Management in High Gear, *Journal of the Operational Research Society,* 57, 475–489.

Xu, L. and Beamon, B.M. (2006). Supply chain coordination and cooperation mechanisms: An attribute-based approach, *The Journal of Supply Chain Management,* Winter, 4–12.

10

Creation and Continuous Development of the Toyota Production System for Solving Current and Potential Business Crises

Shino Hiiragi
Yamagata University

1 Introduction

Toyota[1] has once weathered bankruptcy, which prompted it to create the renowned Toyota Production System (TPS), which in turn has enabled it to remain competitive even under critical business conditions. Specifically, in the post–World War II period, during which the manufacturing of a wide variety of products in small quantities was prevalent, Toyota created a "problem solving" system that enabled it to manufacture automobiles with low cost and high efficiency.

Since then, Toyota has overcome many more challenges, including emissions regulations, trade conflicts, oil price shocks, financial crises, product recalls; man-made disasters such as fires; and natural calamities, such as earthquakes and floods. In this chapter, Toyota's sustainability will be examined through the analysis of its crisis management. In particular, we

---

[1]Toyota's corporate history started with the inauguration of the automobile department of the Toyoda Automatic Loom Works, Ltd. in 1933. Toyota Motor Co., Ltd. was established in 1937, and Toyota Motor Sales Co., Ltd. was separately established in 1950. In 1982, Toyota Motor Co., Ltd. and Toyota Motor Sales Co., Ltd. merged into Toyota Motor Corporation, which is also the company that we know today. In this chapter, we refer to all three entities as "Toyota" for simplicity.

examine how the company withstood various crises over the years and became one of the leading automobile manufacturers today.

In this chapter, we hypothesize that "business crisis management is problem solving." We examine the relationship between external and internal environmental changes, each business management phase, as well as the capabilities needed in each phase. Based on a background analysis of TPS's formation, we review Toyota's organization capability building and crisis management using a theoretical framework and a case study. Specifically, we discuss the company's capability building, based on interviews with Toyota officials[2]; its crisis management, especially its response to the major earthquake in Eastern Japan on March 3, 2011; and the lessons the company learned from that experience, based on a keynote lecture at a recent supply chain management symposium.[3]

2 Definitions of Crisis and Crisis Management

This section proposes hypotheses about the definition of crisis, crisis management, and related capabilities, before proceeding to a case of Toyota's crisis management. While crisis management has numerous definitions, in this chapter, we focus on the view of crisis management as a business management tool (Alison, 1971; Herman, 1972; Quarantelli, 1978; Selbst, 1978; Perrow, 1984; Slatter, 1984; The Academic Association for Organizational Science, 1990, 1992; Oizumi, 1992, 2006; Hiruma *et al.*, 2011). Oizumi's (2006) definition of crisis management is based on the relationship between external or internal environmental changes and the organization's business management.

---

[2]This was from an interview with Mr. Haruyoshi Yamada, Project General Manager at the Toyota Institute of Toyota Motor Corporation on September 2012, and an interview with Mr. Masami Doi, Project General Manager at the Public Affairs Division of Toyota Motor Corporation on October 2012.

[3]The 5th International Supply Chain Management Symposium and Workshop, with the theme, "Building dynamic capabilities across the supply chain: Challenges in the age of complexity and globalization," was held on March 10, 2012. The keynote lecture, "Manufacturing (*Monozukuri*) and Risk Management" was delivered by Mr. Keiji Masui (Managing Officer; Deputy Chief Officer, Purchasing Group, Toyota Motor Corporation) and Mr. Hiroaki Koda (General Manager, Global Purchasing Engineering Department, Purchasing Project Management Division, Purchasing Group, Toyota Motor Corporation).

Hypothesis 1 (Definition of crisis)

> *Crisis is an extreme business risk of failing to respond to rapid and significant external and internal environmental changes.*

The concept of business crisis is expected to expand, including increased sustainability risks such as bankruptcy, dramatic sales decrease, and survival issues. The increasing complexity and globalization has led to greater and more rapid environmental and sustainability risks. Thus, in this chapter, we focus on the increasing importance of business crisis management.

Hypothesis 2 (Definition of crisis management)

> *Crisis management involves suppositions, preparations, correspondences, and provisions for the rapid and significant external and internal environmental changes before and after they occur.*

Crisis management should include specific actions based on organizational identity and capabilities. In this chapter, we identify the organizational capabilities required for business crisis management.

Hypothesis 3 (Definition of organizational capabilities needed for business crisis management)

> *In the correspondences and provisions for a crisis, a company's problem–solving capability must develop the best solution (action) for the situation. The company must also ensure that its identity and leadership go hand in hand to make sure they both are moving in the same direction. To this end, each member of the entire organization should be regularly informed and involved in the company's goals.*

Figure 1 summarizes the relationship among these three concepts. The concepts become even more critical as the changes occur rapidly or in a larger scale. The vertical axis indicates the speed and scale of change, while the horizontal axis indicates the before and after phases of business management action.

Crisis correspondence has a significant aspect that cannot be anticipated. In the figure above, the further out a crisis is, the faster and greater the company's judgment and response. This entails certain organizational capabilities. Efficient judgment becomes even more important when a company has not adequately prepared for a crisis or when the crisis is very

External/ internal environment changes		Business management action plan				
		Before		After		
		Supposition	Preparation	Correspondence		Provision
		Plan		**Do**		**Check/ Action**
Small — Daily Changes = Fluctuations	E x p e c t e d	· Plan & take preventive action	· Plan preventive action & make provisions (Be prepared with alternatives, building a mechanism, preparation, training, etc.)	· Problem solving in status quo (Kaizen) · Daily management as per set standards	Independence Low — Leadership Low	· Continuous Improvement · Innovative ideas · Following upper-level policy · Building problem-solving capability
		· Plan & take preventive action at a manageable level	· Plan preventive action & make provisions at a manageable level	· Problem solving to achieve breakthroughs (Revolution) · Hoshin (policy) management based on business policy · Creating and practicing new ideas		
Unprecedented Changes = Crises — Big	U n e x p e c t e d	Preventive action cannot be taken because the changes are beyond calculation	Beyond physical preparation · Developing problem-solving capability for the management of unexpected crises	· Self-directed judgment and practice based on the business policy in every phase · Creating and practicing new ideas · Individual/organization problem-solving capability and leadership	Independence High — Leadership High	· Formation of problem-solving capability · Business policy as the code of conduct · Grooming Leaders

Fig. 1. Before and after correspondence for external and internal environmental changes, and crisis management.

Source: Authors.

urgent. In such cases, each organizational member's and unit's problem-solving capabilities are required.

On the other hand, such compartmentalized judgment brings about risks beyond the control of that organization. To address such crises, the company needs to ensure each member shares the corporate identity and acknowledges the corporate leadership. In companies, when each organization member becomes move skilled, so does the power to manage them by showing the distance of the organization.

Furthermore, in this chapter, we demonstrate change (risk) management as the plan–do–check–act (PDCA) cycle in total business administration. This change management involves not only suppositions, preparations, and correspondences but also provisions for future challenges, in order to ensure the company's continuous improvement. The lower right corner of Fig. 1 shows that crisis correspondence in the absence of suppositions and preparation does not need physical preparation, but rather building organizational capability. Toyota learned this strategy from its experience and has implemented it in response to subsequent crises. This strategy, known as the TPS, is discussed in detail in Sec. 3.

3   Origin and Subsequent Deployment of TPS

This section discusses Toyota's post–World War II financial crisis (bankruptcy), which was its most significant crisis since the company's foundation. From the viewpoint of building organizational capability, we discuss how TPS was developed by learning from a crisis, and how it has been implemented to solve subsequent crises.

3.1   *Toyota's bankruptcy and lessons learned*

Historical studies on Toyota include those on the formation of TPS, the company's founders, and its start-up cost management strategy (Satake, 1998; Wada and Yui, 2002; Maeda, 2007, 2008; Simokawa and Fujimoto, 2009; Hiiragi, 2009; Maeda, 2009a, 2009b; Wada, 2009). Toyota has also published information on its history (Toyota, 1958, 1967, 1978, 1987, 2012). In this section, we review Toyota's financial crisis (bankruptcy) in the beginning of 1950, which was its most significant crisis since its foundation.

In 1949, to restrain the post–World War II inflation, the government implemented the "Dodge Line" financial and monetary contraction policy as a credit squeeze measure. As a result, the domestic industrial fundraising capabilities in Japan declined. Toyota was significantly affected by this policy and required a 188,200,000-yen bailout by the Bank of Japan. However, the consequences of the Dodge Line policy were very serious, necessitating the company to separate its sales division in order to ease its cash-flow situation, negotiate an ongoing strike with workers for two months, and prompt more than 2,000 voluntary redundancies (greater than the 1,600 originally planned). In addition, Kiichiro Toyoda was compelled to vacate his position as company president.

Toyota averted what could have been the most critical situation owing to an increased demand for automobiles by the U.S. Army, two weeks after the Korean War broke out. By this time, Toyota had learned its lessons from its previous financial crisis and became stronger as a result. Ten years after the financial crisis, it had built and expanded the TPS. Following the motto "safeguard one's own castle" (Ishida, 1968), which means solving one's problems on one's own and not turning to other organizations such as banks for help, it developed a new way to reduce wastage in production.

Figure 2 shows how the TPS concept stemmed from the problem of how to manufacture efficiently given the lack of financial, human, and physical resources. Through TPS, Toyota continues to follow its essential corporate principle, the "Toyota Way" (Toyota, 2001), even as it became a global

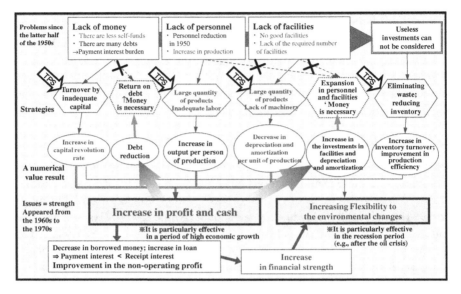

Fig. 2.   Conceptual diagram of Toyota's problems from the 1960s to the 1970s, and how TPS resolved these problems.

Source: Authors.

company with a significant amount of resources. The TPS shows Toyota's adamantine "organization vector," which it developed from the lessons it learned in its major financial crisis.

3.2   *What the TPS brought was the grand sum of problem solving*

A significant number of studies have examined the TPS, Toyota Way, and the Kaizen philosophy on a global basis (Ohno, 1978; Ohno and Monden, 1983; Monden, 1983; Imai, 1986; Ogawa, 1994; Suzuki, 1994; Jonson and Broms, 2000; Hino, 2002; Just-in-time Manufacturing System Collegium, 2004; Liker, 2004; Liker and Meier, 2005; Hiiragi, 2009, 2010; Rother, 2010; Monden, 2011). These studies especially examined the evolution of capabilities in manufacturing (*genba*), specifically manufacturing systems, organizational knowledge, and organizational capability (Nonaka and Takeushi, 1995; Osono *et al.*, 2008; Fujimoto, 1999, 2007), as well as the significance of the TPS during a crisis (Lee, 1999a, 1999b, 2000).

Kaizen is a continuation of the problem-finding and -solving philosophy for present and potential problems. During the TPS building phase, Toyota was facing significant business issues such as the lack of resources due to insufficient capital. Through problem solving in each *genba*, it was able to address these issues. It is important to note that TPS was developed not as a result of a vision, but out of an urgent, special need.

The TPS includes evolving in response to and accommodating changes. The TPS's implementation and way of thinking can be adapted to a particular situation without changing its basic concept. The Toyota business culture believes that "not changing is a bad habit" (OJT Solutions Inc., 2006), which means that one should change as much and as soon as possible. Toyota's business culture of problem-finding and -solving evolves based on the challenges the company faces in its external and internal environments.

The TPS played a significant role in Toyota's global expansion. Studies about Toyota and the Japanese automotive industry in the 1960s and 1970s (Kawahara, 1995; Kamiyama, 2003; Shimokawa, 2009) have pointed out that these periods were times of breakthrough as well as difficulties, as both the company and the industry faced challenges such as emissions regulations, oil price shocks, and voluntary export restraints. The problem-solving capability of the Japanese automotive industry became stronger from this experience, as has been noted by researchers in the 1980s, including researchers from the Massachusetts Institute of Technology (Womack *et al.*, 1990).

3.3   *Problem-solving capability and simultaneous crises coming from increasing globalization and complexity*

The most recent global crises that started with the subprime loans in the U.S. in 2007 and the fall of major global financial institutions such as the Lehman Brothers' in 2008 significantly affected the Japanese automotive industry, actualizing high exchange fluctuation risks and fixed charge ratios. Toyota's performance was profoundly affected, and this period became particularly known as "Toyota shock" (Inoue and Ito, 2009; Shiomi and Umehara, 2011).

During this period, Toyota's rapid and broad crisis management provisions became apparent. For instance, in response to the first significant decrease in performance on November 2008, Toyota adopted "emergency measures to improve earnings launched in autumn 2008, [which] resulted in an improvement of approximately 130 billion yen by March of the following year through implementation of emergency value analysis (VA) activities and limits on investments in facilities" (Toyota, 2012). This was a significant problem-solving task for Toyota.

Another of Toyota's setbacks are its product recalls in the 2000s (Hasegawa, 2001, 2002, 2007, 2010; Yoshida, 2007; Yoshida and Kondo, 2008; Sakurai, 2010; Liker and Jranz, 2011; Liker and Ogden, 2011; Fujimoto, 2011, 2012a, 2012b), which were brought about by the external environmental factor of complexity. Automobile design has become complex, and Toyota's organizational capability building could not catch up with the increasing problem-solving load (Fujimoto, 2012a, 2012b). This issue showed that having sufficient problem-solving capabilities is important (Liker and Ogden, 2011).

4   Organization Capability Building for Dealing with Unexpected Crises

This section discusses Toyota's next problem-solving strategy through the analysis of their crisis management implementation during the earthquake in Eastern Japan in March 2011, and the lessons it learned from this experience.

4.1   *Toyota's lessons from the 2011 earthquake in Eastern Japan*

The readiness of Toyota and its suppliers during the 1997 fire of Aishin Seiki, and the re-establishment of its supply chain management following the 1995 Great Hanshin Earthquake, the 2004 Mid-Niigata Earthquake, and the 2007 Off Mid-Niigata Earthquake demonstrate the problem-solving capabilities of Toyota and its affiliates. The company's response during the 2011 earthquake in Eastern Japan, which was perhaps the most significant crisis the company faced in recent years, also demonstrated the company's capabilities (Shimokawa, 2009; Saeki, 2011; Fujimoto, 2011, 2012a, 2012b). Toyota's response during this disaster is outlined below:

On March 11, 2011, a massive earthquake of magnitude 9.0 occurred with an epicenter off the coast of Miyagi Prefecture at 2:46 pm. Immediately after the earthquake, TMC convened a crisis-response meeting and quickly established a companywide countermeasures headquarters. The order of priorities was established as follows: (1) protecting human life and providing relief to victims, (2) aiding rapid recovery of disaster regions, and (3) resuming production. At the same time, earthquake-response headquarters for each function including procurement, production, and so on were established within each operations group; countermeasures headquarters were established outside the Head Office in Nagoya, Tokyo, and other regions; and a system for the central collection of information using video-conferencing was established (Toyota, 2012).

The above policy was clearly specified by Mr. Akio Toyoda, president of Toyota, who demonstrated strong leadership during the crisis. The organization's actions were based on its basic philosophy and policies. Mr. Masami Doi (Project General Manager, Public Affairs Division, Toyota Motor Corporation) whom we interviewed, described the company president's response during the crisis:

> President Toyoda provided a clear direction on the countermeasures the headquarters needed to take during the aftermath of the earthquake, which aimed to support the entire region regardless of business connection... The Toyota factories were nearly undamaged by the earthquake and thus could continue operating; nevertheless, the president ordered the plants to shut down to ensure the safety of its and its subsidiaries' employees and their families as of March 14, the following Monday. However, this was not the only reason. If the Toyota factories continued to operate, the suppliers, who were affected, may not be able to deliver the materials. We felt uneasy about it.

On March 12, a day after the disaster, "TMC worked with partner companies, including suppliers, as well as dealers to begin the transport of emergency relief supplies, and 60 TMC employees were dispatched to the affected regions as an emergency relief team" (Toyota, 2012). By the evening of March 11, minivans were on their way to deliver aid to affected communities. Toyota's response demonstrates the company's problem solving ability based on its philosophy.

The company also demonstrated its problem-solving capabilities when it assisted one of its suppliers: "In addition, the entire automobile industry worked together for the recovery of Renesas Electronics Corporation, a manufacturer of microcomputers that became a bottleneck in the supply chains of multiple automakers, when its main plant in Ibaraki Prefecture was damaged by the earthquake. As a result, partial recommencement of production, which was initially projected to take place in September, was achieved in June" (Toyota, 2012).

Mr. Hiroaki Koda, general manager of Toyota's Global Purchasing Engineering Department, actively participated in providing field assistance during this time. During a keynote lecture, "Manufacturing (*Monozukuri*) and Risk Management," he described the company's actions following the disaster:

> What enabled us to restore production in such a short time? ... Firstly, we worked by ourselves.... We think that human resource development is the most important factor that enabled us to review the problems and determine what to do when preparing for unexpected accidents that might occur. Our manpower was built based on the *Kaizen* philosophy and activities, which enabled us to solve day-to-day problems in the manufacturing field (*genba*).... In addition, the *Kaizen* spirit and teamwork also made possible our early return to production. I learned valuable lessons from this experience.

Toyota's experience during this disaster enabled it to realize once again that the most important aspect of crisis management is problem solving. Mr. Koda explained:

> I recommended a basic policy for the re-establishment of production... We promised that we would go on, following the thinking that our "own company is last".... As for the earliest re-establishment of the production of Company R (a famous Japanese microchip manufacturer, which has been affected by the earthquake), we had to restore the most difficult part of quality in the manufacturing. We believed that if we could do that, the re-establishment of production should go smoothly and set our priorities.

Mr. Koda led the re-establishment team. His policy, as he explained above, reflects Toyota's corporate philosophy, and offers a glimpse of his strong leadership. His response during the crisis is another excellent example of the link between leadership and problem solving when facing a crisis.

In addition, Toyota reinforced its efforts to completely address its procurement issue. The disrupted Japanese supply chain owing to the earthquake had widely affected the company's overseas business, especially its parts supply: "the number of items regarding which there were supply concerns dropped from a peak of 500 in late March to just 30. In addition to restoring damaged plants, diligent efforts to develop production alternatives and alternative parts and to perform rapid quality assessments at manufacturing sites resulted in a restoration of production that greatly exceeded initial expectations" (Toyota, 2012).

4.2 *Education system for building problem-solving capability*

Even though problem-solving capability is very important, it is not something that can be developed in a short span of time. Toyota's on-the-job training of its employees through the TPS, as well as its off-the-job educational system, is widely recognized. Mr. Haruyoshi Yamada of the Toyota Institute described the company's human resources development efforts:

> In Toyota, there are three human resource units, one of which is the Toyota Institute, which handles corporate learning. Based on the "Toyota Way" established in 2001, we worked on teaching total company learning including how to entrust tasks to our overseas business offices. If the Toyota Way focuses on value, the TBP (Toyota Business Practice) focuses on how to achieve value. We also teach the TCS (Toyota Communication Skill)... Basically every aspect of training at Toyota teaches problem solving.

Figure 3 shows the eight steps of TBP, which resemble those in quality control (QC), with the exception of step 1. In step 1 of the so-called "QC Story (step-by-step improvement in QC)," one chooses the theme and then figures out what is going on.

		Steps	
P	Step 1	Clarification of problem	Clarifying the problem
	Step 2	Understanding the actual condition	Stratifying the problems and identifying the main problem
	Step 3	Setting a goal	Setting a target
	Step 4	Factorial analysis	Identifying the real cause of the problem
	Step 5	Policy proposal	Drawing out proposals for problem-solving
D	Step 6	Proposal implementation	Implementing the proposals
C	Step 7	Examination of the effects	Examining the results and the process of problem-solving
A	Step 8	Standardization	Standardizing and expanding solutions to include other sections

Fig. 3. Eight steps of "Toyota Business Practice" for problem-solving.
Source: Toyota (2012).

This might be because the problem is already apparent in daily *Kaizen* activity. Yamada explained that Toyota had changed step 1 since 2005 in order to emphasize unapparent problems.

This change shows that the level of problem solving is becoming sophisticated as complexity and globalization continues to increase. Although problem solving is as important as before (Ono, 2003; Liker and Franz, 2011), "problem finding" is gradually emerging as a much important step (Roberto, 2009).

4.3 *Toyota's problem-solving capability issue*

Next to problem solving, another important step is discovery. For example, following the 2008 global financial crisis, TMC had already begun considering by May 2010 to restructure its manufacturing structure, including the subsidiary vehicle manufacturers within the Toyota Group. In July 2011, after the earthquake disaster, TMC announced plans for positioning Tohoku as its third production center in Japan, following the Chubu region (central Japan) and the Kyushu region (southern Japan), as well as for helping the Tohoku region recover by strengthening TMC's *monozukuri* (conscientious manufacturing) activities there (Toyota, 2012). According to Mr. Doi, innovative field research significantly improved Toyota's manufacturing capability in the Tohoku district at a much earlier time than would otherwise be possible.

In the problem-solving capability building for responding to changes, self-change is always needed. During his speech at the 7th Toyota World Convention on November 2011, Mr. Toyoda made the following remarks (Toyota, 2012):

> For me, growth means 'continuing to change in response to changes in society'. That is what will make sustainable growth possible. Whether Toyota will be able to continue growing will depend on whether we can keep supplying better cars to customers in the various regions.

The above passage highlights Toyota's next issue. The cases we discussed above show how Toyota's problem-solving capability has contributed to its crisis management. However, in the age of increasing complexity and globalization, greater correspondence and capability are needed. "Problems that are apparent" can be easily solved. However, merely finding "unapparent problems in front of us," is not enough either.

In addition, "completely invisible problems" should be taken into account when determining an organization's overall strategy. This strategy includes change correspondence in the global arena and innovation capability to enable high operational capability. These changes are not only operational capability in daily routines, but rather management powers. In this regard, Toyota's problem-solving organizational capability is expected to further improve.

5 Conclusions and Future Research

In this chapter, based on the assumption that business crisis management entails responding to critical changes, we discussed business problem-solving capability through a case study of Toyota's crisis management. Our key findings are as follows:

1. Problem-solving capability is the most basic aspect of change management.
2. Real-time problem solving is the most important aspect of crisis management, because some crises cannot be anticipated.
3. To achieve real-time problem solving, measures and policies for problem-solving capability building need to be structured.
4. Toyota achieved real-time problem solving through field practice (on-the-job training) and education (off-the-job training).
5. However, in the future, the importance of capability building will increase for business management issues beyond operation level problems.

In this study, we found that Toyota had learned significantly about total business crisis management from its experiences, and has already started to expand their efforts. By observing and analyzing Toyota's subsequent achievements in this regard, we can obtain a clearer definition of the concept of organization capability for future crisis management, which can be further examined in future research.

Acknowledgments

I would like to thank Mr. Keiji Masui, Senior Officer and Deputy Chief Officer, Purchasing Group, Toyota Motor Corporation, and Mr. Hiroaki Koda, General Manager, Global Purchasing Engineering Department, Purchasing Project Management Division, Purchasing Group, Toyota Motor

Corporation, for granting permission to use excerpts of their lecture at The 5th International Supply Chain Management Symposium and Workshop on March 2012. I also thank Mr. Haruyoshi Yamada, Project General Manager, Toyota Institute, Toyota Motor Corporation, and Mr. Masami Doi, Project General Manager, Public Affairs Division, Toyota Motor Corporation, for their cooperation during the interviews.

References

The Academic Association for Organizational Science (1990). Feature, Crisis Management, *Organizational Science*, 23(3) (in Japanese).

The Academic Association for Organizational Science (1992). "Feature, Natural Calamity and Organizational Correspondence", *Organizational Science*, 2(3) (in Japanese).

Alison, G.T. (1971). *Essence of Decision : Explaining the Cuban Missile Crisis*, Boston: Little Brown.

Fujimoto, T. (1999). *The Evolution Manufacturing System at Toyota*, London: Oxford University Press.

Fujimoto, T. (2007). *Competing to Be Really, Really, Good: The Behind-the-Scenes Drama of Capability-Building Competition in the Automobile Industry*, Tokyo: I-House Press.

Fujimoto, T. (2011). Supply chain competitiveness and robustness: A lesson from the 2011 Tohoku earthquake and 'virtual dualization', *MMRC Discussion Paper Series* No. 354 (in Japanese).

Fujimoto. T. (2012a). Virtual dualization of supply chains: Dealing with tradeoff between competitiveness and robustness, *Organizational Science*, 45(4), 25–35 (in Japanese).

Fujimoto, T. (2012b). *Regeneration Based on Monozukuri: the Field Doesn't Lose against Appreciating Yen and Earthquake Disaster*, Tokyo: Nihon-Keizai-Shinbunsha (in Japanese).

Hasegawa, Y. (2001). Reconsidering the theory of target costing: Costs generated by recalls of Japanese auto-manufacturers, *Reitaku-Keizai-Kenkyu*, 9(1), 37–51 (in Japanese).

Hasegawa, Y. (2002). Product performance of leading Japanese automobile manufactures: With reference to the analysis of recall data, *Reitaku-Keizai-Kenkyu,* 10(1), 29–44 (in Japanese).

Hasegawa, Y. (2007). A milestone to a theory of cost-caused recall: A feedback from a recall report of automobiles in both U.S. and Japan, *Reitaku-Keizai-Kenkyu*, 15(1), 93–113 (in Japanese).

Hasegawa, Y. (2010). Impact of automotive recalls and "recall cost" issues, *Reitaku-Keizai-Kenkyu*, 18(1), 67–75 (in Japanese).

Herman, C.F. (1972). *International Crisis: Insights from Behavioral Research*, New York: Free Press.

Hiiragi, S. (2009). Accounting suitable for the Toyota Production System: Feasibility of the fair performance evaluation, PhD Dissertation No. 7, Aichi Institute of Technology (in Japanese).

Hiiragi, S. (2010). Accounting to make effective use of 'genba power' — For the fair performance evaluation and implementation of total management control. *Journal of Society for Social Management Systems.* Available at: http://management.kochi-tech.ac.jp/ssms_papers/sms10_112%20Shino%20Hiiragi100309%20final.pdf. (1st Apr. 2013)

Hino, S. (2005). *Inside the Mind of Toyota: Management Principles for Enduring Growth*, New York: Productivity Press.

Hiruma, Y., Hada, Y., Meguro, K. and Kondo, S. (2011) Adaptation to environment and kaizen of local government officials of Niigata Prefecture on crisis management — Case of the 2004 Mid-Niigata earthquake and the 2007 Off Mid-Niigata earthquake, *Institute of Social Safety Science Collection of Papers* No. 14 (in Japanese).

Imai, M. (1986). *Kaizen, The Key to Japan's Competitive Success*, New York: McGraw-Hill.

Inoue, H. and Ito, H. (2009). *Toyota Shock*, Tokyo: Kodansha (in Japanese).

Ishida, T. (1968). *Safeguard One's Own Castle*, Tokyo: Kodansha (in Japanese).

Jonson, H.T. and Broms, A. (2000). *Profit Beyond Measure: Extraordinary Results through Attention to Work and People*, Denver: Free Press.

Just-in-time Manufacturing System Collegium (ed.), (2004). *Just in Time Production System*, Tokyo: Nikkan Kogyo Shinbun (in Japanese).

Kamiyama, K. (2003). Overseas activities of Toyota Motor Corporation, *Journal of Political Economy*, 70(2–3), 1–21 (in Japanese).

Kawahara, A. (1995).*Essence of Competitiveness: Fifty Years of Japanese and American Automobile Industries*, Tokyo: Diamond (in Japanese).

Lee, J.-H. (1999a). Lean production system and the function of finished car company in crisis: A case study of the correspondence to the fire of Aishin Seiki, *Keizai-Ronso*, 163(5–6), 572–590 (in Japanese).

Lee, J.-H. (1999b). Lean production system and flexibility of working in the crisis, *Keizai-Ronso*, 164(2), 45–65 (in Japanese).

Lee J.-H. (2000). Flexibility of Toyota Production system in the crisis and inter-firm relations, PhD Dissertation, Kyoto University (in Japanese).

Liker, J.K. (2004).*The Toyota Way*, New York: McGraw-Hill.

Liker, J.K. and Meier, D.P. (2005).*The Toyota Way Fieldbook*, New York: McGraw-Hill.

Liker, J.K. and Franz, J.K. (2011). *The Toyota Way to Continuous Improvement*, New York: McGraw-Hill.

Liker, J.K. and Ogden T.N. (2011). *Toyota Under Fire, How Toyota Faced the Challenges of the Recall and the Recession to Come Out Stronger*, New York: McGraw-Hill.

Maeda, J. (2009a). The formation of Toyota System and its significance (1), *Mita-Shogaku-Kenkyu*, 52(4), 13–39 (in Japanese).

Maeda, J. (2009b). The formation of Toyota System and its significance (2), *Mita-Shogaku-Kenkyu*, 53(1), 39–55 (in Japanese).

Maeda, Y. (2007). A study about history of cost management in Toyota Motor Corporation, PhD Dissertation, Hitotsubashi University (in Japanese).

Maeda, Y. (2008). The production system and cost management consciousness of Toyota at the time of founding, *Melco Journal of Management Accounting Research*, 1, 21–32 (in Japanese).

Monden, Y. (1983). *Toyota Production System: Practical Approach to Production Management*, Norcross, GA, USA: Industrial Engineering & Management Press, IIE.

Monden, Y. (2011). *Toyota Production System: An Integrated Approach to Just-in-time,* 4th edn, London: Taylor & Francis.

Nonaka, I. and Takeuchi, H. (1995). *The Knowledge-Creating Company: How Japanese Companies Create the Dynamics of Innovation*, London: Oxford University Press.

Ogawa, E. (ed.) (1994). *A Study of the Toyota Production System*, Tokyo: Nikkei Inc. (in Japanese).

Ohno, T. (1978). *Toyota Production System: Beyond Large-Scale Production*, Portland: Productivity (in Japanese).

Ohno, T. and Monden, Y. (eds.) (1983). *New Development of the Toyota Production System*, Tokyo: Japan Management Association (in Japanese).

Oizumi, K. (1992). Basic concepts development for corporate crisis management : Theory building as to decision-making & organizational behaviors, *Journal of Business Research*, 13, 15–26 (in Japanese).

Oizumi, K. (2006). *Crisis Management General Theory*, Tokyo: Minerva-Shobo (in Japanese).

OJT Solutions Inc. (2006). *Toyota's Favorite Phrase*, Tokyo: Chukei Publishing (in Japanese).

Ono, T. (2003). *Working in Lean Production System: Based on Participant Observation on Automobile Plant*, Tokyo: Ochanomizushobo (in Japanese).

Osono, E., Shimizu, N. and Takeuchi, H. (2008). *Extreme Toyota: Radical Contradictions That Drive Success at the World's Best Manufacture*, Hoboken: Wiley & Sons.

Perrow, C. (1984). *Normal Accidents: Living with High-Risk Technologies.* New York: Basic Books.

Quarantelli, E.L. (1978). *Disasters: Theory and Research*, Thousand Oaks: Sage Publications.

Roberto, M.A. (2009). *Know What You Don't Know*, New Jersey: Pearson Education.

Rother, M. (2010). *Toyota Kata: Managing People for Improvement, Adaptiveness, And Superior Results*, New York: McGraw-Hill

Saeki, Y. (2011). Japanese manufacturing renaissance and present issues: Discussion about automobile SCM and TPS, thorough the correspondence for the earthquake in Eastern Japan, *Ritsumeikan-Keieigaku* 50(2–3), 57–80 (in Japanese).

Sakurai, M. (2010). The aftermath of Toyota's recall to the corporate reputation, *Kigyo-Kaikei*, 62(8), 66–76 (in Japanese).

Satake, H. (1998). *The Generation, Development, Transformation of Toyota Production System*, Tokyo: Toyo Keizai (in Japanese).

Selbst, P. (1978). *The Containment and Control of Organizational Crises*, Sutherland, JW (Ed.), Management Handbook for Public Administrators. New York: Van Nostrand Reinhold.

Shimokawa, K. (2009). *Automobile Industry: The Structure of Crisis and Rebirth*, Tokyo: Chuokoron-Shinsha (in Japanese).

Shimokawa, K. and Fujimoto, T. (eds.) (2009). *The Birth of Lean*, Cambridge: Lean Enterprise Institute.

Shiomi, H. and Umehara, K. (2011). *Toyota Shock and Aichi Area Economics: Toyota Folk Tale and Actuality*, Kyoto: Koyo-Shobo (in Japanese).

Slatter, St. P. Slatter (1984). *Corporate Recovery: A Guide to Turnabout Management*, London: Penguin.

Suzuki, R. (1994). *Japanese Production System and Business Society*, Sapporo: Hokkaido University Press (in Japanese).

Toyota Motor Co., Ltd. (1958). *Toyota: 20 Year's Company History* (in Japanese).

Toyota Motor Co., Ltd. (1967). *Toyota: 30 Year's Company History* (in Japanese).

Toyota Motor Co., Ltd. (1978). *Toyota: 40 Year's Company History* (in Japanese).

Toyota Motor Co., Ltd. (1987). *Toyota: 50 Year's Company History: "Unbounded Creation."* (in Japanese).

Toyota Motor Corporation, (2001). Toyota Way 2001. Available at: (http:// www.toyota.co.jp/jp/csr/principle/toyotaway2001.html). (01 Nov. 2012)

Toyota Motor Corporation, (2012). Toyota 75 year's company history. Available at: (http://www.toyota.co.jp/jpn/company/history/75years/index.html.)

Wada, K. and Yui, T. (2002). *Biography of Toyoda Kiichiro*, Nagoya: The University of Nagoya Press (in Japanese).

Wada, K. (2009). *An Allegory of Manufacturing; From Ford to Toyota*, Nagoya: The University of Nagoya Press (in Japanese).

Womack, J.P., Jones, D.T. and Roos, D. (1990). *The Machine That Changed the World: The Story of Lean Production*, New York, Macmillan Publishing Company.

Yoshida, E. (2007). Dilemmas between high quality and low cost: An analysis of Japanese automobile recall data, *Mita-Shogaku-Kenkyu*, 49(7), 47–61 (in Japanese).

Yoshida, E. and Kondo, T. (2008). Automobile recall and target costing, *Kigyo-Kaikei*, 60(5), 108–115 (in Japanese).

Index

3PI activities, 55
4 + 1 Big module concept, 140

account receivable, 89
accounting treatment of
   compensation funds, 9
Act on Compensation for Nuclear
   Damage, 4
Act on Emergency Measures
   Concerning Damage from the
   March 2011 Nuclear Accident, 19
active business crisis management,
   102
activity map, 134
added value yielded by each
   stakeholder acting alone, 26
agency, 25
aggravated Nissan's business
   problems, 66
allocated burden, 25
alternative dispute resolution, 34
ambivalence, 98
Amoeba management, 43
analog to digital paradigm shift
   period, 50
analog to digital shift, 60
apparent and uncontrollable threat,
   99, 100
Articulated Hauler, 130
Asian currency crisis, 52
attractiveness, 143
attractiveness by differentiation, 128
attributed loss, 25

balanced scorecard (BSC), 79
bankruptcy, 97

bankruptcy proceedings, 31
Barnard's organizational equilibrium
   theory, 22
benchmark, 90
benefit of a particular member acting
   alone, 23
Body-on-frame, 137
boundary systems, 120
burden charges, 7
burden of consumers, 17
burden of creditors, 16
burden of employees, 19
burden of local governments, 19
burden of shareholders, 15
burden of suppliers, 19
burden of TEPCO and its
   management, 20
business crisis management, 97,
   101–105, 166
business domains, 85
business lifecycle, 93
Business Plan, 11
Business Portfolio Management, 57,
   93
business profit, 89
business structure strategy, 11, 72
business value, 93

capacity-usage ratio of facilities, 140
Capital Cost Management (CCM), 83
capital efficiency, 88
capital injection, 7
cash flow of segment, 85, 92
cash flow shortages, 31
cash on hand and at banks, 89
causes of business crises, 100

CFT pilot, 70
CFTs of Nissan, 70
characteristics of CFTs, 69
chassis, 137
Closed Custom Parts Suppliers from Network, 126
closed modular parts, 138
Closed Module-parts Suppliers from Network, 127
CMF, 139
CO_2 emissions, 89
coalition of individuals, 22
cockpit, 139
commissioner, 9
common components, 137
common industry module, 141
common module family, 138
company with auditor, 20
company with average profitability, 26
company with committees, 20
compensation scheme based on market principles, 8
compensation system, 58
competitive power of merchandize, 138
complexity, 171
Comprehensive Special Business Plan, 11
concrete contents of NRP, 71
constitution of CFTs, 70
continuous flow of production, 125
Contract for Indemnification of Nuclear Damage Compensation, 5
cooperative game theory, 23
core platforms, 137
corporate goal, 98
corporate rehabilitation law, 33
Corporate Reorganization Act, 8, 14
corporate revitalization, 31
corporate value, 91
cost basis, 17
cost efficiency, 143
cost leadership strategy, 135
cost of invested assets, 89, 92

cost rate of invested assets, 89
cost ratio on total revenue, 24
cost-reduction efficiency, 128
crisis, 97, 98
crisis boundary management, 109, 118, 120, 121
crisis management, 101
cross-functional team (CFT), 66
crystal cycles, 51
Cuban Missile Crisis, 101

damage liability, 3
debtor in possession (DIP), 33
Declaration of Frankfurt, 55, 59
definition of quality, 56
design of simultaneous engineering, 141
desired amount of return, 24
Development Bank of Japan, 32
development stages of modular parts, 128
direct causes, 100, 105
division net profit, 90
double standard model, 109, 115, 117–119, 121

Efficient solution, 144
Electricity Business Act, 17, 18
electricity price, 7, 17
Electronic Architecture, 140
emerging countries, 137
endogenous counterparts, 105
engine compartment, 139
Enterprise Turnaround Initiative Corporation of Japan (ETIC), 14, 34
EVA®, 88
Ex ante disaster management, 150
exchange rates, 109, 111, 112, 114–118, 121
exogenous causes, 105
exterior and interior parts, 137

Facilitation Fund Act, 5
fair compensation, 17

fair costs, 17
fair profits, 17
fair rate of contribution, 23
fairness to electricity users, 17
Family Group, 139
FF, 136
fiduciary, 25
financial and non-financial measures, 79
financial structure strategy, 11
fire of Aishin Seiki, 172
five stakeholders, 10
fixed costs problem, 100, 105
foreign investment, 89, 92
frameless construction, 137
free cash flow, 89
front-underbody, 139
Frontier curve, 144, 145
full cost method, 7, 17, 27
full-line strategy, 146

Genba, 170
general burden charge, 7, 10
generation-transmission split, 20
global alliances of parts suppliers, 143
global purchasing, 141
global sourcing, 131, 141
globalization, 110, 111, 121, 171
grand coalition, 23
Great Hanshin Earthquake, 172
group rationality, 24, 26

hastily formed network, 153
hybrid supply chain, 126, 143
hybrids of stage 1 and stage 2 modules, 141

IMF monetary crisis, 49, 53
impairment accounting, 36
improved cost efficiency, 141
indirect causes, 101, 105
individual rationality, 24, 26
insolvent, 8
intangibles, 91
interest earned, 89

interest paid, 89
internal capital system, 90
internal interest system, 90
internet, 156
inventory, 89
invested assets, 89
item cost ratio on total revenue, 26

JAL philosophy, 44
Japan Airlines, 14, 31
Japan Air System, 31
Japanese governance structure, 20
joint benefit, 23
joint contribution amount, 24
joint losses, 27
Just-in-Time production system, 125

Kaizen-costing, 136
Kaizen philosophy, 170
Kazuo Inamori, 43
keiretsu network, 141
Kunhee Lee, 50, 54, 59
Kunhee Lee's ownership, 59

lagging indicators, 78
latent threat, 99
leadership, 167
leading indicators, 78
lean production system, 125
LED, 86
Lee's ownership, 59
levers of control, 120
liquidation business crisis management, 102, 103

major earthquake in Eastern Japan, 166
Management Approach, 85
management by objectives, 92
Managing Division, 38
March 11, 2011, 172
marginal profit, 91, 92
Market for the less wealthy customers, 144

Market for the middle class
    customers, 144
Market for the wealthy customers,
    144
market in, 60
Marugoto, 86
matrix organization, 129, 134, 141
matrix performance evaluation
    systems, 79
Mid-Niigata Earthquake, 172
mismanagement at a turning point,
    99, 105
mixture of stages 1 and 2, 141
modular design in the matrix, 130
modular designs, 141
modular furniture design, 134
modularization, 132, 141
module costing, 130, 141
modules differentiated among
    automakers, 138
modules in stage 1, 141
Monocoque, 137
Moriarity's Allocation Formula, 24,
    26

nation's bankruptcy, 21
negative contribution, 24, 25
negative incentives, 24
net profit before tax, 89
Nissan 180, 68
Nissan GT 2012, 68
Nissan Power 88, 69
Nissan Revival Plan (NRP), 67
Nissan value up, 68
Nissan's CFT management, 66
Nissan's common module, 140
no-fault unlimited liability, 8
Non-dominated solutions, 144
Non-inferior solutions, 144
Nuclear Damage Liability Facilitation
    Fund Act, 4–6, 13
nuclear power plant operators, 7

Off Mid-Niigata Earthquake, 172
off-the-job educational system, 175

on-the-job training, 175
open common modules, 138
Open Custom Parts Suppliers from
    Market, 127
Open Module-parts Suppliers from
    Market, 127
operating profit, 89
opportunity cost, 24
optimal supply-chains, 145
Organic Electro-Luminescence
    (OEL), 86
organization's survival, 22
organizational capability, 170
organizational efficiency, 22
organizational equilibrium, 22
organizational knowledge, 170
outsourced parts, 138
overall equipment efficiency, 92
overall supply-chain, 146
overcapacity, 100

packet communication, 156
Panasonic, 83
Pareto Improvement, 144
Pareto Optimum Points, 144
partial coalition, 23
partners' voluntary fund
    contributions, 159
partnership with Renault, 67
parts commonization, 137
performance evaluation system, 78
personal innovation, 55
personnel expenses, 91
physical distribution costs, 91
Platform, 136
potential threat, 99
pre-disaster management, 150
preventive business crisis
    management, 102, 103
problem solving, 165
problems with CFTs, 71
process evaluation measures, 78
process innovation, 55
product differentiation, 138
product innovation, 55

product mix, 91
product-out, 60, 61
profit management model, 109, 115, 118, 121
profit plans, 109, 115–117
provision of compensation funds, 7
purchasing matrix, 135

QC Story, 175
quality control (QC), 175

radioactive contamination, 3
ratio of design commonization, 140
reactive business crisis management, 102
rear-underbody, 139
reasons for Nissan's success, 66
reduced losses, 27
reduction in number of auto-parts suppliers, 138
relationships between process evaluation measures and result measures, 78
relationships between the CFT and V-up programs, 77
repulsive business crisis management, 102
repulsive crisis management, 103
residual income, 90
Resona Holdings, 14
restructuring expenses, 84
result measures, 78
return on assets, 92
return on sales (ROS), 88
risk, 103
risk management, 103, 104
robust supply chain, 128
Route Marketing, 38

sacrificed value caused by each stakeholder acting alone, 26
sales credit, 92
Samsung Electronics, 49
SANYO, 83
scale economy, 133

scale merit, 138
self-controlling management, 58
share the burden, 3
shareholder value, 88
shareholder's equity, 89
sharing the burden, 4
Sharing the burden of TEPCO's restructuring, 13
side payments of incentives, 22
side payments of negative incentives, 25
Silicon cycle, 51
simultaneous crises, 171
smart-phones, 52
Social Costs of Kapp, 25
social responsibility of the manager, 22
special dues, 8, 10
special loss, 9
special profit, 9
stakeholders, 10
standard working capital, 90
strategic matrix, 131
strategic parts, 137
strategy map, 92
strongest supply-chain, 145
structural adjustments, 53
structural-component modules, 139
structural-components (mechanisms), 139
sunk costs, 84
suppliers' network, 138, 143
supply chain management, 172
synergy effect, 27
synergy effect generated by the grand coalition, 24

target costing, 133, 136, 143
TBP (Toyota Business Practice), 175
TCS (Toyota Communication Skill), 175
TEPCO public assistance scheme, 6
TEPCO's restructuring, 10

The Innovation Network Corporation of Japan, 86
Theory on the Fair Allocation, 21
third-party allocation, 32
three types of supply-chains, 146
TNGA, 136, 137
Tokyo Electric Power Company (TEPCO), 3
Toyoda Automatic Loom Works, 165
Toyota, 109, 110, 113–118, 165
Toyota Institute, 175
Toyota New Global Architecture, 136
Toyota Way, 170
trade-off ratio, 144
transmission & distribution company, 20
turnaround, 3
turnaround procedure after bankruptcy, 14

turnaround procedure before bankruptcy, 12, 14
two goals of the hybrid products, 143

unique optimal balance, 145
utility function, 144, 145

value-creating process, 133
value engineering, 133
vertical systematization, 57
V-Fast team's activities, 76
visible but controllable threat, 99
Volvo Strategic Make or Buy matrix, 141
Volvo's matrix organization, 130
V-up program, 74
V-up team, 75
V-up team's activities, 75

weakest supply-chain under the disasters, 146